Good Homes magazine

101 BEDROOMS

Published by BBC Worldwide Ltd
Woodlands
80 Wood Lane
London W12 0TT

First published 2002
Copyright © BBC Worldwide 2002
All photographs © *BBC Good Homes
magazine* 2002

ISBN 0 563 53442 7

Edited by Alison Willmott

Commissioning Editor: Nicky Copeland
Project Editor: Sarah Lavelle
Book Design: Claire Wood
Design Manager: Lisa Pettibone

Set in Amasis MT, ITC Officina Sans,
New Baskerville
Printed and bound in France by
Imprimerie Pollina s.a. - L86915
Colour origination by
Kestrel Digital Colour, Chelmsford

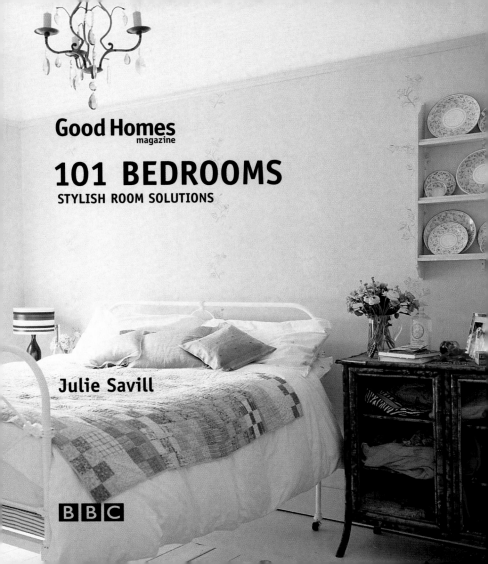

Good Homes magazine

101 BEDROOMS

STYLISH ROOM SOLUTIONS

Julie Savill

BBC

CONTENTS

INTRODUCTION

It's your dressing room, the place where you relax, maybe where you read or watch TV. You spend eight hours a night here, that's a third of your life, so doesn't your bedroom deserve some careful and quite special planning? While your sitting room is the public face of your home, a place that maybe needs to be pet and child friendly, your bedroom is the most private area and it's here that you can suit yourself entirely when it comes to the decorating. If you have kept the downstairs cool and pale you can afford to indulge in layers of bohemian velvets and silks in rich purples and pinks. Or perhaps you have a yen for Hollywood glamour that you haven't quite had the nerve to make reality in the sitting room. Now is your chance ...

Whether you are changing just the wall colour or going for a top-to-toe makeover, your first job is to decide on the look you want to end up with. If you have existing pieces of furniture or a carpet that the new scheme needs to include, a mental picture of what you are aiming for will help make sure you get the bedroom of your dreams. And that is the purpose of this book – a style guide to steer you to a scheme that suits you and your home. It is usefully divided into sections devoted to different looks, from the cool, unclut-tered Contemporary to the clever and money-wise Budget. Even if you feel you already know your style I would recommend looking through all 101 looks as you may be surprised by what you find, and by what you feel about rooms that are outside your normal decorating range. Be adventurous. If you normally live with barely-there shades and the minimum of items on display, pause over the pictures filled with rich colour and carefully collected objects. Open your mind. If you prefer green to blue but like the overall look of a room switch the colours in the picture for those you feel at ease with but keep to similar tones, depths and proportions of colour to ensure success.

Of course, decorating is not simply a matter of colour and you will need to consider the floor coverings, window treatments and furniture. Storage is a major issue in a bedroom and should be one of your priorities. With the best will in the world it is impossible to keep a room organized and tidy if there are no designated places for your belongings to live. Off-the-peg solutions are the simplest and some of the bigger DIY and decorating stores now sell excellent bedroom furniture in a wide range of styles at very affordable prices. If you are feeling a touch more creative, buying second hand and stripping, adding your own paint finishes and replacing door and drawer handles will give you unique results for a few pounds.

Finally, don't forget the finishing touches, the things that turn an ordinary bedroom into a haven. Fresh flowers are the heroes of the day so don't deny yourself the pleasure of a handful of blooms in a simple vase or jug. Keep photographs and small collections around to remind you of special times. Then all you need to add is your favourite music and soothing scents to complete the transformation. Enjoy!

Julie Savill, Editor
BBC Good Homes magazine

The look: With French-style furniture and shutters at the window, this room has a continental feel. It sets traditional furniture against a plain, contemporary backdrop of calming colours to create a simply styled but elegant look.

Colour: Powdery blue-grey walls create a serene air that's ideal for a bedroom. For a look that really soothes the senses, choose a carpet in the same colour, but a tone or two darker so that it 'grounds' the scheme.

Bedlinen: Pure white bedlinen adds a refreshing touch to brighten the dusky atmosphere at the same time as enhancing the moodiness of the blues by providing a crisp contrast. Lace-edged or embroidered white bedlinen scores high for classic style – these simple pillowcases are stitched with a large floral design.

Furniture: The bed is the centrepiece of the room, its cane frame and carved wooden detailing evoking an air of French-style elegance. This classic theme is continued by the two tables, one in dark wood and the other in light marble. The textured quality of the cane and the mixture of light and dark tones among the furniture add interest to the plain and simple scheme, and the grey tones of the marble echo the wall colour.

Window: Shutters have always been popular in mainland Europe, so they create a continental air as well as providing a stylish window treatment. The louvred variety allows plenty of light through and can be folded back individually, offering as much flexibility as curtains. Wooden shutters can be painted in any colour to match your scheme.

The look: The cream and plum colour scheme and elaborate window treatment give this room its firmly traditional character. The classic look is big on comfort, so be generous with fabric in lavish drapes and upholstered furniture.

Colour: If you plan to get fussy with soft furnishings, keep your colour scheme simple. Softer than white yet coolly elegant, rich cream is perfect for a classic look. The room's only other colour, a dark traditional plum, is used sparingly.

Pattern: A scheme dominated by a single colour needs pattern to liven it up, and checks and stripes keep the look formal rather than fussy. Wallpaper with a smart narrow stripe brings subtle interest to the walls, while plum checks add colour and pace when used for the smaller soft furnishings.

Window: The dramatic cream drapes are purely for decorative effect – checked blinds lined with blackout material keep out light at night. The heavy curtains have a pleated pelmet heading and are held back by tiebacks. Plum-coloured bobble braid highlights the curved shape of the tiebacks and pelmet.

Furniture: You don't need antique furniture to follow through a traditional look – just use fabric and colour to make pieces fit your scheme. A valance hides the base of the divan bed, and checked fabric covers the bedside table and padded headboard. A cream finish makes the tall chest of drawers look at home – if you can't find furniture the right colour, try painting pieces to suit.

BEDROOM TIP
When decorating in period style, look for inspiration in paintings or pictures from the era you're interested in, or visit historic houses furnished in that style

The look: If you like the romance of decorative furniture but don't want to go completely classical, take your cue from this room. The ornate bed and wall sconces sit well with a colour scheme of cool contemporary lilacs and clean white bedlinen.

Colour: One way of introducing colour without it overwhelming a room is to use it on just one wall. The paler lilac on the far wall keeps the overall look light and spacious, while the darker shade provides a richer backdrop for the decorative iron bed-head and candle sconces. The white duvet cover enhances the light atmosphere, its sparsely embroidered sprays of lavender echoing the wall shades. Two of the cushions and the candles introduce touches of warmer colour, as accents of dusky pink and deeper damson.

Furniture: The cast-iron bed was made by a local craftsman – if you can afford it, having furniture custom-made will ensure that you get a unique piece designed just as you want. However, similar beds are available in the shops. With a simple backdrop you can get away with an eclectic mix of furniture – the bedside tables are basic folding designs bought at a bargain price.

Accessories: The iron candle sconces are the work of the craftsman who made the bed. When the candles are lit, the mirrors reflect the flames to create an ultra-romantic atmosphere. The gallery of photos adds a personal touch. Small individual pictures may look lost on a large wall, but grouping several together creates an effective display. The gilt frames unite them and add a hint of glamour.

The look: Natural materials against a white background are essential elements of the colonial look. For a truly tropical flavour, fill your room with solid wooden furniture and leafy palms, and fit louvred shutters to filter the midday sun.

Colour: Painting the walls, shutters and wardrobe in white gives the large room a beautifully airy feel. In this light atmosphere, the mellow wood tones of the drawer unit, chair and flooring give off a warm glow, while the darker oak chest adds depth to the scheme. The earthy brown of the bedcover and the leaf greens of the throw and plants continue the natural theme.

Shutters: Wooden shutters are perfect for a continental or colonial look, and make a versatile treatment for a large bay window. Fitting separate sets to cover its upper and lower halves allows you to keep the bottom ones closed for privacy while opening the top to get the full benefit of bright early morning light. Louvred shutters also come with adjustable slats so that you can regulate the amount of light that filters between them.

Fabrics: As well as choosing appropriate colours, look for fabrics with natural fibres and ethnically inspired designs, such as this Indian-style bedspread. And don't forget animal prints – a sure-fire way of defining colonial style.

Accessories: If you've inherited some battered trunks or suitcases, the colonial room is the perfect place for them. If not, a hatbox covered with stickers from exotic destinations conveys the idea of a traveller's retreat. Lush green palms in big wicker pots bring the jungle indoors.

The look: Although the blue and white colour scheme is clean and contemporary, the antique furniture and traditional-style details give this room more than a hint of classic inspiration.

Colour: The blue that covers the walls creates a fresh, airy atmosphere, although a cool, pale colour like this may create a chilly feel if you have a high-ceilinged room. The white window dressing, carpet and bedlinen keep the look light, and against this ethereal backdrop the black iron of the decorative bed frame looks particularly striking. Dark wood furniture adds a touch of warmth.

Window: A simple sheer curtain panel is a contemporary window treatment, but has been given a slightly more classic feel by draping it across the window and tying it back at one side. The black metal curtain pole echoes the iron bed frame.

Furniture: Period-style furniture needn't cost the earth – your local junk shop can yield some bargains. The small wooden cabinet and wall mirror (from an old dressing table) are junk-shop buys that cost just £8 in total. Salvage yards are another good source of old-fashioned furnishings, such as the radiators in this room. The iron bed is from an antiques shop.

Accessories: Carefully chosen accessories can add character to a room, but don't be too much of a slave to style – a mix of modern, traditional and personal adds a homely feel. The dried roses started life as a Valentine's day present, and were later mounted and framed. The old cream-coloured telephone was found in a skip.

CLASSIC

The look: An atmosphere of classic comfort pervades this room, with its luxuriously upholstered bed, heavily draped curtains and mound of cushions in sumptuous fabrics and rich colours.

Colour: A harmonious combination of pinks and browns in soft, muted tones creates a warm and relaxing atmosphere. It's important to include a mixture of different shades in any room. Here the palette starts with the pale plaster effect on the walls, then moves on via the rosy pinks of the bed upholstery and curtains to the dark wood of the furniture and the rich reds and golds of the cushions.

Walls: The walls have the mottled and textured effect of old plaster. This has been created by applying a plaster finish, which is available from specialist paint stores, and then painting over it with a mixture of scumble glaze and raw umber artist's acrylic paint.

Bed: A lavishly upholstered bed with a thickly padded headboard and swagged footboard will give the plainest room a luxurious feel. The patterned fabric, button detailing and swag effect are all clearly traditional in style. For extra comfort, pile the bed high with cushions and bolsters covered in opulent, jewel-coloured fabrics, such as silks, velvets and brocades. For traditional finishing touches, trim them with gold braid, fringing or tassels.

Curtains: Generously draped curtains also typify classical style. If your window is big enough to take it, choose a patterned fabric featuring a large design – damask or brocade is ideal. Add big tassel tiebacks and a decorative swag at the top.

BEDROOM TIP
Decorative trims are essential finishing touches for classic-style soft furnishings. Get the look with tassels, bobble braid and fringing – stitch them to curtains and cushions for instant traditional looks

Colour: Sunny yellow, a real feelgood colour, creates an enlivening contrast with the imposing black iron of this room's original fire surround. It also tones with the beigey background colour of the hearth tiles. Painting the walls above the picture rail white, to match the ceiling, increases the impression of space and height in the room. The all-white bedlinen and curtains freshen the atmosphere further, and the ruched bedcover adds textural interest to the scheme.

Window: French doors that afford a garden view are an enviable feature in a bedroom, so don't hide them away under heavy curtains. These are dressed with light double drapes: an old striped bedspread cut to size is layered with filmy muslin. Both dressings hang from simple clips which offer an instant window-dressing solution – they grip onto the top of the curtain panels without requiring any sewing at all.

Furniture: The black iron bed echoes both the colour and the straight lines of the fireplace. An old wooden dressing table, covered with a lace-edged runner and topped with a battered old mirror, evokes a feeling of faded elegance.

Accessories: Unusual accessories, such as the Moroccan pendant light shade and the puppet that hangs from the bed post, add character to the room. The amber and green glass of the shade picks up on the colour of the fireplace tiles. The subtle pinks and oranges of the pictures tone with the yellow walls, while adding accents of blue and green, and their gilt frames introduce a hint of glamour.

BEDROOM TIP
Before you start to search for curtain fabrics, look around your home for sheets, tablecloths or throws that might do the job. Hung using pincer clips, they make instant no-sew curtains. Napkins and tea towels also work well at smaller windows

The look: This room draws on the aristocratic chic of a French château for a look that's blissfully romantic and thoroughly feminine. Airy colours and graceful furniture with shapely curves are its key elements, while a sparkling glass crystal or two doesn't go amiss.

Colour: Colours are kept pale for that look of faded grandeur, and the mix of ice-cool pastels has romantic appeal. The lightest wash of eau-de-nil green highlights the neutral backgrounds of the various fabrics.

Soft furnishings: Toile de Jouy, with its traditional two-colour pastoral scenes, is the fabric most evocative of this style. Another classic, smartly striped ticking, varies the pattern pace. Layer your bed with toiles of different colours for a light-hearted interpretation of the look. A bed canopy is a must, but you don't need a four-poster – simply drape a length of striped voile over a dowelling rod suspended by cup hooks from the ceiling. Trim the edge with a row of tinkling crystals, and add a flourish to your curtains too, with a heading of ribbon bows.

Furniture: Metalwork can't be too curvy for this style, so choose the prettiest iron bed you can find. Slightly battered paintwork on wooden furniture gives a comfortably lived-in feel, so you could create the look on a modest budget by decorating and distressing bargain buys from junk shops. Search for pieces that have shapely lines, and paint them in pale colours.

Accessories: For lighting, think ornate metal wall sconces or chandeliers. Add tall candles for romance, plus a small selection of delicate glassware to keep the crystals company.

The look: This room harks back to the 1930s, with polished wooden floorboards and period-style fireplace and furniture. The light colour scheme adds a refreshing touch to its nostalgic style.

Colour: A calming combination of blue and green complements the wood tones of the flooring and furniture. The walls are colourwashed in pale blue, and the picture rail picked out in lime green, which is also used on the large cupboard. Plain white bedlinen keeps the look simple and fresh, while accents of bright blue and black strengthen the scheme.

Colourwash: For a light colourwash, first apply a base coat of white emulsion and leave to dry. Mix a little scumble glaze with your top colour, then paint it over one small area at a time, spreading it with large brush strokes and allowing some of the base colour beneath just to show through.

Furniture: It is the furniture that evokes the 1930s feel. The owners had the iron bed made to their specifications, and its black frame echoes the inner part of the fire surround. The wooden chest of drawers gives off a well-polished gleam, just like the floorboards.

Accessories: Pictures from the era add depth to a period style – the old seaside poster brings the look alive with its glimpse of a 1930s scene. The pot plant enhances the natural feel created by the wood surfaces. If you want to display books, make sure there is adequate shelf space, otherwise they will add clutter rather than desirable character.

Colour: A palette of gentle natural tones gives this small bedroom a restful feel, while working to increase the illusion of space. Although white is the best colour for making a tiny room feel light and airy, softer neutrals a tone or two darker will create a more relaxing look that's easier to live with, especially in a bedroom where a tranquil atmosphere is often high on the wish-list. Use these shades for background features such as the walls and curtains, then, if you feel the need to freshen things up a bit, choose mainly white bedlinen.

Windows: Neat roller blinds in a fine, pale-coloured fabric provide privacy during the day, while long curtains shut out bright light when needed, as well as giving the windows a softer look. Contemporary style is added by details such as the small square cutouts on the blinds and the simple tab-top heading of the curtains. Wooden curtain poles fit in with the natural theme of the room.

Radiator cover: A wooden cover conceals the radiator and, in a room with no windowsills, also provides a handy ledge for display or storage. Purpose-made radiator covers have decorative grille fronts with fretwork or cutout designs to allow the heat through. Those made of wood or plain MDF can be painted to match your scheme.

Fabrics: Natural fabrics such as cotton, wool and linen suit a neutral scheme. Add interest with a variety of textures rather than colours. In this room, texture comes from the herringbone-weave curtains as well as the cable-knit cushion and the pile of woven towels.

The look: If you want a bedroom that's glamorous without being girly, opt for subtle greys. This is a look designed to appeal to both sleeping partners, with a monochrome masculine colour scheme forming a sophisticated backdrop for romantic accessories and sensual fabrics.

Colour: The walls are covered in a light pewter shade, the colourwashed finish softening its effect. The black iron bed stands out smartly against this cloudy background, while plain white bedlinen lightens the look. For a truly relaxing scheme, avoid all bright colour and choose only muted tones that won't outpace the walls – the cushions here add subtle accents of plum, olive and darker grey.

Furniture: For classic romance, choose painted wooden furniture and an iron bed, but keep the sophisticated feel with relatively plain designs – no fussy scrolls or carved detailing. For a restful feel, paint furniture in pale pastels rather than white – the table beside the bed is decorated in a light blue that tones with the walls.

Soft furnishings: Use fabrics to add glamour; silk and velvet cushion covers complement classic white cotton bedlinen. Look for textures that add an element of pattern without disturbing the plainness of the scheme. Keep window dressings light and airy – the tall window is dressed with a gossamer-fine panel of white-spotted voile.

Accessories: With a few well-chosen finishing touches you can indulge your romantic side without undermining the overall look. A cut-glass Venetian mirror frame with curvy edge and etched flowers makes a beautiful feature for the wall, while a beaded frame and storage box sparkle on the bedside table.

BEDROOM TIP
To give your bedlinen a seductive scent, sprinkle your sheets with a little rose or lavender water

The look: High ceilings and a big bay window are shown off to full effect by fresh colours and pared-down furnishings. Bright yellows and clean white increase the airy feel of the room, while simple roller blinds enhance the shape of the bay.

Colour: When planning colour schemes, many of us focus on one room at a time, rather than coordinating the whole house. However, if you have many rooms opening off a landing, you could end up with ugly clashes. A simple way of easing colour flow is to use different shades of a single colour. If you love yellow, start with a bold shade on your landing walls, then use a lighter tone in the bedroom. Vary the tones within the room too – here the duvet cover features a third, paler shade. By including enough tonal variation, you can get away with using just one colour in your bedroom or even your whole house.

Floor: White-painted floorboards make an already light scheme twice as bright. Prepare clean sanded boards with a coat of primer, then apply a paint specially formulated for floors to ensure a hard-wearing finish. When this is dry, add a coat of protective varnish.

Windows: If you're lucky enough to have big, beautiful bay windows, it's a shame to hide away their shape under gathered curtains. Roller blinds are a less obtrusive option and are, of course, also cheaper as they require much less fabric. Fine white cotton blinds not only suit the simplicity of this scheme but also help to enhance its airy atmosphere.

The look: This bedroom shows a fascinating juxtaposition of classic and contemporary styles, with daringly modern use of strong colour contrasts bringing new life to the original period features such as the leaded window and picture rail.

Colour: Tangerine and blue create an electrifying contrast, and it's a combination that works because they are complementary colours. This is the name given to any two shades that appear on opposite sides of the colour wheel – the tool interior designers use to plan their schemes. Although very different, they intensify and bring out the best in each other rather than clashing. The vibrant tangerine echoes the coloured diamond shapes at the top of the leaded window. The picture rail is picked out in a deep turquoise, while several different shades of blue and aqua feature in the bold checks of the bedlinen.

Window: Painting the window frames in a strong colour is an effective way of drawing attention to the attractive leading. Dark blue velvet curtains add a luxuriously traditional feel alongside the brighter tones of the modern bedlinen. The curtain colour is repeated as accents in the picture and lampbase.

Carpet: The grey carpet introduces a paler tone to offset all the bright and dark colours in the room. A flecked design is a practical choice for a carpet as it doesn't show marks and dirt as easily as a plain one.

Accessories: The accessories reflect the room's old and new theme. An antique sewing machine table and clock sit comfortably in the mix alongside the boldly checked duvet cover and the contemporary print above the bed.

The look: Italian neoclassical style inspired the flamboyant decor in this bedroom, which proves that grand looks needn't have a price tag to match. Ingenious DIY has created a bed fit for an emperor, as well as a set of impressive curtain holdbacks. Plaster pillars, busts and urns are dotted around to complete the look.

Colour: Rich cream and regal red create an opulent backdrop, and are used on different walls for maximum impact and contrast. A line of black ribbon running around the top of the walls echoes the striped cushions and other black accents in the room to give a unified feel.

Floor: Brown Victorian floor tiles blend well with the wood effect on the bed. The bold modern design of the black and white rug may seem incongruous but it adds a touch of fun, as well as bringing the neoclassical decor bang up to date.

Bed: The sleigh bed may look like an expensive buy but is actually made from MDF. To give the look of quality wood, it has been decorated with cream emulsion followed by a top coat of scumble glaze mixed with raw sienna artist's acrylic paint.

Window: If you have wide windows to dress and want grand style on a budget, choose a cheap fabric that you can afford to use in vast amounts. Here, plain natural calico has been sewn up into gathered curtains. The disc-shaped holdbacks are made from circles of MDF covered with a spiral of sash cord, which is glued in place. They are decorated with black and gold paint.

BEDROOM TIP

Gathered curtains should be at least one-and-a-half times as wide as the area you want them to cover. Aim for twice the width if you want a fuller effect or are using fine fabric

The look: Pristine white walls and bedlinen create a pared-down setting for traditional furniture made from dark wood and iron. The result is a smart monochrome scheme that offsets elements of classic charm with a refreshing contemporary atmosphere.

Colour: White walls create a light backdrop for the darker, more traditional elements of this room, such as the wooden door and dressing table. Accents of peacock blue run throughout the room to add a restrained touch of colour – it peeps out from beneath the bedcover and runs in fine lines up and around the walls to highlight the picture rails and door frame. The floor, however, holds a colour surprise in store. Although only just visible in the picture, it is painted in a dazzling sea green.

Furniture: It is the old-fashioned furniture and fittings such as the wooden door and picture rail that determine the classic character of the room. The black iron bed and large dark wood dressing table are both solidly traditional in style, and are thrown into sharp focus by the stark white background. The wide mirror on the dressing table reflects light from the window opposite, helping to enhance the room's bright, airy feel.

Bedlinen: The room's whitewash effect continues with the mainly plain bedcover, although its quilted design adds a spot of textural interest. The gingham border of the quilt and the floral designs on the cushions soften the look a little as well as adding colour.

The look: Vibrant terracotta sets these walls on fire, but their warmth is cooled by lashings of pure white. The powerful contrast between these two colours is bold and contemporary in nature, but the original fireplace and old-fashioned accessories give the room a more classic feel.

Walls: The hot terracotta shade has been applied as a colourwash to give it a softer look. For a dark and dramatic effect, first apply a base coat of full-strength emulsion and leave to dry. For the wash, dilute a paint that's a shade or two darker with between 12 and 20 parts water to one part emulsion, depending on the strength you want. Test the effect on paper first, then apply the wash to the wall in rough crisscross strokes using a 50mm-wide brush. When this is dry, add a second coat using a 100mm brush.

Furniture: In a scheme with both modern and classic influences, an eclectic selection of furniture looks perfectly at home. The wood and wicker items give a comfortable, lived-in feel, and distressed pieces suit the look well.

Window: A simple full-length panel in sheer white fabric allows through plenty of natural light, ensuring that the room feels bright despite the warming effect of the terracotta. A bobble edging gives the plain curtain a more decorative look.

Accessories: Curly wrought-iron accessories in different colours – a black lampbase, copper-coloured wall sconce and verdigris-effect candle-holder – evoke classic style. They are complemented by the finish of the mirror frame, an effect achieved by using a heat gun to strip layers of paint.

BEDROOM TIP
Applying a strong, stimulating shade as a colourwash gives it a less solid effect, making it more relaxing to live with. The broken colour has a 'distressed' look, as if faded with age, which can work well with older or traditional furnishings

The look: The filmstar decadence of Hollywood can be recreated in the bedroom with touches of glitzy gold and silver and expensive-looking fabrics. The generously sized bed is piled with cushions and throws in sensuous silks and furs, creating a look that's steeped in luxury.

Colour: The basic scheme is sophisticated, using shades of cream, camel and ivory to make a neutral contemporary backdrop. Added to this are fun elements of glitz and glamour; the wall beside the bed is decorated with squares of silver leaf. Real silver leaf may be pricey, but aluminium gives a similar effect – both are available from craft shops. Reflective surfaces provide glimmer, with plenty of glass in furniture, mirrors and vases, and accessories with metallic or lacquered finishes.

Bed: The keyword here is big – choose a kingsize bed with a high headboard upholstered in a luxurious material such as suede or leather. These materials are usually as costly as they look, but affordable and realistic fake alternatives are available from fabric stores.

Bedlinen: The silkier the better! White and pale neutrals work best for sheets and pillowcases, but the bed is strewn with cushions and throws made from luxurious fabrics in glamorous shades of pale gold. The decadent feel is emphasized with a few animal-print and fake-fur cushions.

Carpet: A plush or velour carpet in an extravagant shade of pale cream adds luxury underfoot. A furry deep-pile flokati rug is ideal for sinking your bare toes into first thing in the morning.

BEDROOM TIP
Carpet adds instant comfort, and as a bedroom is not a heavy traffic area you can get away with a light colour or luxurious texture that might not wear well elsewhere. If you prefer floorboards, top them with a few cosy rugs to pamper bare feet

The look: Shimmering metallics are at the centre of this look that's full of subtle modern glamour. The glimmer of silver and pewter combines with cool blues and dusky greys to create a calming, contemporary bedroom.

Colour: Painting the walls in the same smoky blue shade as the carpet gives the room a tranquil feel and makes a strong, sophisticated backdrop for the silvery tones of the furnishings. The skirtings are decorated with silver paint, and the front wall is papered with a metallic-effect wallcovering.

Soft furnishings: A glistening floaty voile panel and piles of cushions made from silk, velvet and organza add to the luxurious feel. Look for pale blues, greys and silvery shades in these fabrics to reinforce the metallic theme. The deep plum colour of the bedlinen shows up the lighter cushions and throws on top.

Furniture: A chrome bed with clean lines helps to define the contemporary character of the room, while the curvy writing desk adds a touch of old-fashioned elegance. Bought as unpainted MDF, it was decorated with undercoat, and a light grey satinwood, then finished with metallic varnish mixed with sparkle dust. A stool covered in silvery fabric makes a comfy perch at the end of the bed.

Accessories: As finishing touches, look for shiny steel vases and beaded or metallic picture frames. Personalize a plain wooden mirror frame by painting it in a shade of blue-grey, then stencil on squares with silver paint, or apply silver leaf. Add sparkle to a plain wall with a large canvas decorated using metallic paints.

Loft conversion: If you want a bigger bedroom, look upwards. Converting this loft created a bedroom with the charm of sloping ceilings and plenty of floor space. Before going ahead with a conversion, approach your local authority to find out whether you need planning permission. If done well, a loft conversion can add significantly to the value of your house, so it's worth seeking the services of an architect to plan and oversee the job.

Windows: Loft rooms often lack natural light, but fitting skylight windows in a sloping roof can solve that problem – the three big windows in this room make it feel bright and airy.

Colour: Choosing pale cream for both the walls and carpet maximizes the room's light atmosphere. While the fitted furniture is in a blond wood so that it fades into the background, the dark wood of the more characterful freestanding

pieces teams with the deep plum shade of the bedcover to add warmth to the pale scheme.

Fitted furniture: Lofts are often full of awkwardly shaped corners and angles, but the made-to-measure cupboard and drawer units make use of every nook and cranny to provide versatile storage tailored to the owners' needs.

Texture: A mix of different textures adds interest to the plain furnishings. The trendy waffle-weave carpet provides comfort underfoot, while the bedcoverings combine a luxuriously plushy bedspread and cosy corduroy cushions with cool cream pillowcases in embroidered silk and smooth cottons.

BEDROOM TIP
Units custom-made to fit your bedroom provide generous storage capacity and make efficient use of space. Bedroom design companies offer a high level of service, including a free consultation at your home, and will organize the design, delivery and fitting of the units

The look: The shades of a springtime woodland create a fresh-from-the-country look, with bluebell mauves and blossom pinks alongside leafy greens. Plain colours and subtle patterns give an air of contemporary simplicity, with a hint of romance introduced by the bed canopy and heart-embroidered duvet cover.

Colour: Greens sharpen the sweetness of the lilacs and pinks to form a refreshing, vibrant colour scheme. Using the palest of greens on the walls gives a restful effect as it's similar in tone to the subtle shades of the bedding and bed canopy. Accents of zingier green form a stronger contrast, while the rich bluey mauves of the ribbed cushion and fluffy rug add depth.

Bed: The bed is a timeless design that is unfussy enough for a contemporary setting but has a four-poster frame that could be swathed in elaborate drapes for a more classic look. Here its dressing is simple, with a panel of airy lilac and white voile offsetting the black iron of the bed.

Bedlinen: Layers of linen, quilts and blankets in mauve, lavender and rose bring colour and comfort to the bed. The mix of prints and embroidery enhances the feminine feel of the pastels. The pink cashmere blanket and cushion add a touch of softness among the crisp cottons, while the quilted bedspread has textural interest.

Accessories: The accessories continue the colour and pattern themes of the room, with a chair painted in lilac, a leaf-design lampshade and a print showing a spray of mauve flowers. The best finishing touch of all is the vase of real, fresh blooms.

The look: An all-neutral scheme will give a thoroughly contemporary look, but a minimalist backdrop needn't mean missing out on comfort. While the cream-coloured walls and furniture maximize the feeling of light and space, a big squashy eiderdown and woollen throws and cushions add inviting warmth and texture to the bed.

Furniture: If you want a neat, modern look, choose furniture with clean, simple lines in colours or materials that blend into the background. The bed headboard and chest of drawers match the cream walls almost exactly, while transparent accessories, such as the lampbase, are both contemporary in style and great for maintaining an uncluttered feel.

Bedlinen: By introducing the only colour among the expanse of cream, the eiderdown, woollen throw and cushion make their comfy textures the focal point of the room. In a plain scheme, texture is vital for adding interest. Their sober but relaxing shades of brown continue the neutral theme. The basic bedlinen is in cool cream cotton.

Lighting: Light fittings are often overlooked but can be as important for adding style as fulfilling their function. The distinctive rectangular fitting, in an eye-catching position above the bed, enhances the room's modern character. The bedside lamp provides additional light for reading.

Accessories: Glass accessories and reflective surfaces add to the light, airy feel. A glass lampbase, a collection of paperweights, and vases with simple shapes introduce a hint of modern glamour. The unusual curvy mirror frame adds an individual touch, and as it is in cream, fits the scheme perfectly.

The look: If you want a look that's light and contemporary but also luxuriously cosy, set the scene with an alluring combination of pale colours and shimmering surfaces, then add comfort and personality with textured fabrics and a mix of furniture styles.

Colour: A light backdrop of pale greyish-lilac walls combines with reflective metallics to create an airy room with contemporary glamour. Cushions in muted shades of blue, pink and lilac add warmer, more inviting colour without disturbing the calming environment, and tactile textures such as crushed velvet and fake fur add a cosy side to the room's sophisticated character.

Furniture: A modern mix of wood and metal furniture gives an eclectic, lived-in look. The metallic bed frame, wooden bedside table and colonial bamboo chest of drawers all have character of their own, yet sit happily together.

Bedcoverings: The bed is the comfort focus of the room, topped with a lined throw in luxurious fake fur and piled with cushions in a mixture of feel-me textures. Cream or ivory bedlinen gives a cosier look than pure white.

Wallhanging: A shimmering sheer panel hung on the wall reinforces the glamorous feel of the room and makes a modern alternative to a bed canopy. To create one, use iron-on webbing and an eyelet kit, both from haberdashers. Cut sheer fabric to length, adding 6cm for the hem. Hem the top edge using iron-on webbing, which gives a stronger edge than sewing. Measure six evenly spaced points for eyelets and fix them in place. To hang, fix hooks to the wall to correspond with the eyelet holes.

CONTEMPORARY

The look: White-painted floorboards and a palette of fresh, light neutrals give this room an airy, Scandinavian feel. The look is clean and contemporary but also relaxed and comfortable. Stylish fitted wardrobes that suit the scheme contribute to the minimalist look by keeping clutter under control.

Colour: Wall-to-wall white guarantees a light, bright atmosphere but can seem cold and clinical. For a scheme that's easier to live with, paint your walls in off-white, then soften the look further with furnishings in pale natural tones. Here the light wood of the cupboards, cream curtains and caramel-coloured throw do the trick, and a mat in a light beige breaks up the expanse of white floorboards.

Wardrobes: A versatile self-assembly storage system provides ample cupboard space to keep the room looking uncluttered. This build-it-yourself system allows you to buy as many flatpack frames as you need, then choose doors and fittings from a wide range of styles. The doors are made from pine and pine veneer, and have leather handles. Large banks of plain wardrobe doors can look boring, but the attractive woven effect turns these into a focal point.

Bedlinen: In a plain scheme, even the smallest decorative details catch the eye – embroidered sprays of flowers on the white bedlinen introduce a pretty touch. The grey silk cushion adds glamour, and the beige throw gives the bed a more comfortable appearance.

Accessories: Keep clutter to a minimum, but choose a few accessories that enhance the casual, contemporary feel, such as the canvas storage boxes and laundry bin and the aluminium alarm clock.

BEDROOM TIP
If you can't decide between freestanding and fitted wardrobes, consider how long you're likely to stay in your present home. If you plan to move a lot, freestanding furniture may be more cost-effective as it can go with you. Some self-assembly systems can also be dismantled and moved

Doubling up: A sofa bed is an essential buy for a living room that doubles as a bedroom. If you have to use it every night, look for a sprung mattress and a steel frame. Whether you're buying a sofa bed or a proper bed, always test it out by lying on it. A sofa will give a little over time, so don't be put off if it feels firm to start with.

Furniture: A screen is useful for hiding bedding by day, and by night converts quickly to a stylish hanging space. To make a simple screen, hinge together four pieces of 50 x 200cm furniture-board. Add a length of dowelling for the clothes rail, then decorate the screen with silver paint. The small side tables have also been given a coat of silver paint.

Colour: Calming blues and naturals help the transition from light, contemporary living space to restful bedroom. A summery shade of turquoise covers the walls, while the ceiling and decorative coving are painted white to give the illusion of height and space.

Bedlinen: Blue and white checked bedlinen creates a fresh feel. If you use a sofa bed constantly you probably won't want to pile it with cushions, but you can use the pillowcases to add colour instead.

Blind: A window that's tall but narrow needs a simple treatment that won't block out too much light during the day. A Venetian blind allows light levels to be controlled more easily than with curtains; look for a wooden one to complement the natural tones of the sofa upholstery and polished floorboards.

BEDROOM TIP
Mood lighting helps to switch a room from sitting to sleeping. One way of changing that bright glare to a softer evening glow is by fitting dimmer switches, which give you easy control over light levels. Always switch off the mains power before starting work

The look: A steely mono-chrome colour scheme is a sophisticated backdrop for delicate sheer curtains and romantic accessories such as flowers and candles, resulting in a look that's pure cutting-edge glamour.

Colour: Grey might not be many people's first choice for their bedroom walls but this relaxing shade of pewter works surprisingly well. If you want to give it a try, make sure your room has enough natural daylight to offset any possible gloomy effect. For a strictly monochrome look, stick to pure white for most of the soft furnishings, adding just an accent or two of darker grey to vary the tone. In this room the only colour comes from the painting on the wall; even the flowers and candles are white.

Metallics: The metallic feel of the pewter wall colour is carried through to the furniture and accessories. The bed frame is made of iron, its wavy design offsetting the hard greys to bring out the elegant, feminine side of the scheme. The candlesticks and the frame of the floorstanding vase are also in grey metals.

Fireplace: A fireplace without a surround gives a clean, con-temporary look and, with the alcove painted in a contrasting colour to the walls, remains a notable feature. However, it is simple enough not to vie for attention with the colourful painting above, the focal point of the room.

Window: Lightening the look in more ways than one, sheer white curtains provide privacy without shutting out natural daylight. The floaty quality of the full-length drapes also enhances the romantic feel of the overall room scheme.

Colour: For a feminine bedroom, think pink – but stick to plain furnishings if you want to avoid a look that's too flowery. Bright berry shades look sophisticated and summery, while lilac adds a cool, fresh feel. Plain pink and lilac bedlinen keeps the look tailored. If you want to include a hint of pattern, look for pillowcases with embroidered detailing or cushions with subtle designs in one or two colours.

Wall stripes: Horizontal stripes running around the walls are a good way of introducing different shades of pink, and they also add a geometric element that saves the scheme from seeming too girly. To make the stripes look lively rather than regimented, paint them in varying widths.

Floor: Berry shades look extra tasty when teamed with cream or white. The floorboards are painted in white satinwood to match the shutters and other woodwork, and a lilac diamond border has been added around the edge to echo the bedlinen colour. A coat of silk varnish gives a protective finish.

Furniture: White furniture is great for a clean, contemporary look, and if the surface is distressed it adds a lived-in feel. For casual chic, choose small, freestanding pieces with character rather than big fitted wardrobes. Wicker baskets evoke that feel of easy living, and are handy for storing smaller items such as toys or baby clothes.

Window: Solid shutters and café-style blinds give the window a continental feel. Blinds of this type are ideal if their main purpose is to provide privacy, as they cover the window to eye level without shutting out any light from the top half.

The look: Cool colours and clean lines create a light, contemporary look. The bedcover and cushions add elements of pattern and texture to make the sparsely furnished room more livable.

Colour: A pale icy blue covers the walls, with bands of warmer lilac higher up to add interest. The pale green duvet cover and fresh white throw ensure that the colour temperature remains cool, but a straw-coloured carpet provides warmth underfoot. The accents of plum and terracotta in soft furnishings and accessories add welcome tonal variation.

Soft furnishings: Making your own soft furnishings allows you to give a room a unified look without relying on coordinated ranges bought off-the-peg. Choose fabrics in all the colours of your scheme and combine them to make a luxurious throw and a pile of cushions to add an air of comfort to your bed.

A laundry bag makes another decorative feature for a bedroom, as well as providing useful storage for bits and pieces. The striped fabric adds a hint of pattern to the scheme, while the dark plum shade provides a rich contrast with the lighter colours.

Furniture: Totally unfussy furniture reinforces the room's modern character. Beside the basic bed frame is a tall metal standard lamp with a paper shade, while the wheeled chrome and wood trolley serves as a mobile bedside table. The plain open shelf unit provides a storage and display area alongside a pair of stylish wall hooks.

BEDROOM TIP
Cushions piled on a bed make even the coolest room feel more cosy and inviting. Dress up basic envelope-style covers with buttons, tie fastenings and other decorations

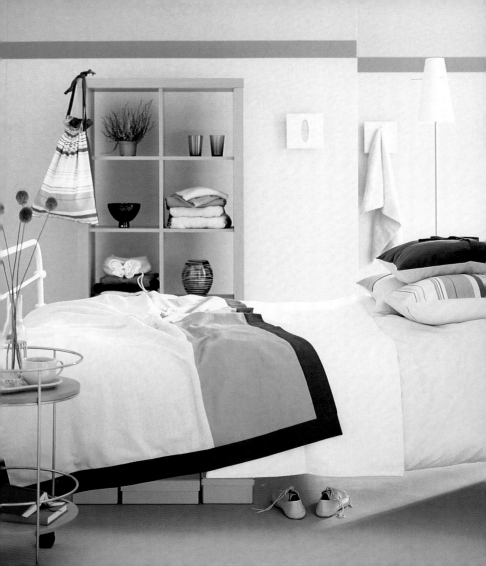

The look: An attic bedroom complete with late 19th-century fireplace makes a surprising setting for a look based on Japanese minimalism. A calming colour scheme, clean lines and oriental furnishings are its key ingredients.

Colour: Unassuming creams and greys sum up the simplicity of oriental style, while flashes of richer colour bring out its more exotic side. The cream-coloured wash on the walls tones with the marble of the fireplace, deftly incorporating this original feature into the scheme. The floorboards are decorated with grey acrylic-based floor paint.

Walls: A clever paint effect gives the walls the look of rice paper. Apply a coat of cream emulsion followed by a wash in a sandy shade, applied using a soft brush. When dry, run a sander over the surface.

Furniture: A futon is the obvious choice of bed for a Japanese theme. The mattress is covered in blue drill to tone with the grey floor. Throws and cushions with jewel colours and glamorous textures add a hint of luxury. The shiny cushion and throw are made from rayon velvet. Other furniture has been kept to a minimum – just two bedside tables and a rack at the end of the bed. These simple timber pieces fit in with the pared-down style of the futon.

Accessories: Minimalist style means keeping clutter under control, and a Japanese-style screen hides a multitude of sins. Oriental accessories such as the wallhanging, pebbles and porcelain bowls in plain, natural colours enhance the room's calm character, and tatami mats double as spare mattresses when friends come to stay.

BEDROOM TIP
An oriental theme lends itself to the simplest of storage solutions – a clothes rail concealed by a Japanese-style screen. This is also a great idea if your budget won't stretch to a wardrobe or if you can't fit one in an awkwardly shaped room

The look: Rich rose-red walls dominate this room, but the emphasis is on earthy tones and natural textures as well as bold colour statements. The white bedlinen, the blond wood of the bed frame and the light, floaty window treatment add a fresh feel which is highlighted by contrast with the warm red backdrop.

Soft furnishings: It's natural all the way for the fabrics, with cotton bedlinen and cushions made from loose woven linens and slubby silks. These materials work best in pale shades that show off their texture – soft pinks and pale beiges lend the room a natural, earthy feel.

Natural dyes: If you can't find fabrics in the colours you want, try dyeing unbleached, untreated cottons and linens using your own natural dyes. Experiment with materials from your garden or vegetable rack – the fabrics here were dyed using berries, onions and red cabbage! Simply boil your dye stuff in water to create a rich colour, then immerse the fabric. The results won't be colourfast though, so make sure you keep them out of a mixed wash.

Window: Give your window an original and interesting look by hanging three separate sheer panels in different colours side by side. The panels are dyed in natural pinks and oranges that echo the colours of the cushions.

Furniture: The simple pine bed enhances the natural theme. The blue-painted side table adds a cool accent that intensifies the richness of the red wall.

The look: With dark wood furniture in a restrained cream setting that would do justice to Japanese minimalism, this room has elements of oriental influence but does not appear too themed. Flashes of hot pink and purple lift the look onto a slightly more exotic plane, adding colour without overwhelming the overall air of contemporary cool.

Colour: The pale cream walls and carpet blend seamlessly to create a light backdrop for the rich brown furniture and deep fuchsia accessories. As the largest area of colour in the room, the blind puts the spotlight on the tall window. The pink open-faced blooms scattered across the white bedlinen temper the plainness of the scheme with a touch of modern flower power.

Furniture: Ranges of dark wood furniture imported from Asia and India can be found in many high-street stores, and look as much at home in a plain contemporary setting like this as in a more ethnically styled room. If you want to play up the oriental feel slightly, look for pieces with rattan panelling, like the headboard of this bed.

Blind: The subtle two-tone design of the blind fabric echoes the rattan of the headboard. The plain border that trims its lower edge adds greater emphasis to the window, balancing the dark tones of the furniture with a deeper shade of pink.

Accessories: The casual use of fuchsia and purple in incidental accessories – suede-covered albums and tulips – dabs the important accent colours around the room. A line-up of unfussy, good-looking boxes turns the lower shelf of the console table into a tidily organized storage area.

BEDROOM TIP
If you have a blind that's too short for your window – perhaps because you've brought it from your previous home – adding a border can make it fit. Choose a fabric of a similar weight to the main part of the blind

Colour: This contemporary room shows how shades of one colour used together can create a successful scheme. Colour is confined to the walls and teamed with plain white furniture for a bold, clean-cut look. The mid-tone pink on the fireplace wall creates a bright but warm feel, while the darker stripes on the window wall add depth and further colour interest to the scheme.

Wall stripes: Horizontal stripes have the advantage of making a room feel wider. However, they also appear to lower the ceiling, so don't use them unless your room is tall. This ceiling is painted white to maintain a feeling of height. If you paint a wall with stripes in a range of shades, start at the bottom with the darkest and use a lighter shade for each following stripe as you work upwards.

Furniture: White furniture forms a fresh contrast with the deep pinks. The white fire surround matches the furniture and stands out against the background to make an eye-catching focal point. If your room is large enough, place a single bed at an angle for a more offbeat look.

Bedlinen: The main bedcoverings are kept light and subtle to avoid drawing attention away from the coloured walls. The duvet is a very pale pink with a white spot design. The sprig-print and purple cushions add dots of pattern and colour accent.

Window: Elaborate window dressings would look too fussy against the striped wall, so the narrow sash window is simply dressed with a panel of sheer white organdie hanging from a nickel pole.

BEDROOM TIP
If you need more privacy than sheer curtains can provide, or can't sleep with moonlight shining through them, consider fitting a blind made of blackout fabric. A slim roller blind can be fixed unobtrusively within the window recess so as not to spoil the delicate look of your sheers

The look: Contemporary but comfortable, this room combines simple modern furniture with cool but livable blues and lilacs and prettier touches such as the carved floral headboard.

Colour: If you need to make a small room feel more spacious but are keen to use colour, decorate with cool hues such as blues or greens. These appear to recede, making the space seem larger. In this room soft blues, greys and lilacs in closely toning shades create a tranquil scheme, which is freshened by plenty of white.

Window: While cool colours can give a stuffy room a fresher feel, they may also seem a little too chilly, so make sure there is plenty of natural daylight to counteract this effect. Choose a light curtain fabric, and extend your pole or track beyond the sides of the window so that the drapes hang over the walls when they are drawn back without shutting out any light from the window.

Carpet: In a cool-coloured bedroom, you may want to boost the comfort factor by fitting a warm and cosy floor-covering. Choose a carpet in a mid-tone that harmonizes with your other colours, such as this slate-grey Wilton.

Furniture: All-white furniture keeps the look light. In general, the lines are clean and contemporary, but the magnificently carved headboard of the wooden bed pretties up the plainness alongside the simpler pieces and injects a touch of character. The tall paper light shade is another distinctive feature. Grey wicker storage boxes at the end of the bed add a relaxed feel.

The look: A mix of natural tones and textures creates a relaxing contemporary look. The geometric lines of the furniture and the hardwood window treatments add a more masculine mood.

Colour: For a calming all-neutral scheme, use a range of different shades – from cream and coffee to darker caramel and chocolate – on the walls, bedlinen and accessories. The striped bedlinen introduces pattern and pace without compromising the room's masculine feel. Don't go overboard with lively designs in a neutral scheme; instead use texture to add an element of subtle pattern, as in the ribbed throw and cushion and the wicker laundry basket. The wood tones of the furniture, flooring and blind continue the natural theme, while accents of black add definition to smarten up the overall look.

Wall checks: Painted checks in a range of natural tones make a feature of the chimney breast. Measure up and draw out your checks on the wall, using a plumbline and spirit level to make sure the lines are straight. Before masking off the squares and painting them, make a plan on paper showing which shade should go where to ensure that you get a pleasing overall effect.

Floor: For a restful bedroom, use the same colour on the floor as on the walls – the wood-effect flooring tones closely with the caramel paint shade on the window wall.

Window: You don't need flowing drapes to give a window a dressed look. Solid shutters, painted to match the woodwork, flank the tall windows, while the wooden Venetian blinds echo the orange tones and slatted headboard of the bed.

BEDROOM TIP
Hanging a blind at a tall, narrow window will help to improve its proportions, especially if you keep it lowered part of the way. Curtains, on the other hand, will cover the sides of the window and emphasize its narrowness

The look: Clean white, light blue and a total lack of clutter give this room a modern, ultra-airy look with a seaside-fresh feel. In true minimalist style, furniture is limited to a bed and two wooden chairs.

Colour: Pure white predominates, with the floorboards painted to match the walls and the bed also shrouded in white. In such a light environment, dark wood furniture really stands out. The use of the light blue shows how painting just one wall a different colour can give a room a totally new dimension; it not only adds welcome colour to the stark white surroundings but also makes a feature of the far wall.

Allergy watch: This room was designed with an allergy sufferer in mind: smooth painted floorboards and light cotton bedlinen don't harbour dust mites like thick carpets and heavy quilts. Help to banish them from bedding by airing your mattress regularly. If you are allergic to feather bedding, try polyester hollow-fibre or wool-filled pillows.

Cupboards: In a minimalist scheme, fitted storage keeps clothing and other clutter out of sight. Panelled wooden doors fit in with the easy-living mood of the room, and blend in with the wall when painted in the same colour. Stretching all the way from floor to ceiling, their giant size makes them look dramatic.

Picture: The big abstract picture adds colour and interest to the white wall. It was made by enlarging a photograph at a copy shop, then sticking the copy to the wall with PVA glue. Rubbing with an emery board gives a worn look.

Making space: Crafty storage solutions and foldaway furniture made this 2.8 x 3.4m box room into a multipurpose space. It's normally used as a home office, but when guests come to stay the wall-mounted desks fold down to allow space for a sofa bed to be unfurled, turning it into a spare bedroom in a matter of minutes.

Storage: Deep shelves extend along the whole of the wall above the desks to provide plenty of space for files and books. Storage boxes that stack neatly on top of each other make the most of the vertical wall space. Bamboo edging gives the shelves a decorative finishing touch. On the floor near the window, more storage boxes are ideal for stashing away out-of-season clothes.

Colour: Deep purple is a brave choice for such a small room but, as a colour that promotes an atmosphere of calm, it is appropriate for an office area. To enhance the natural tones of the bamboo, the shutters, shelves and other woodwork were painted in a pale green.

Window: The purple walls might have overpowered the room if it wasn't for the abundance of light that floods through the tall window. The simple window treatment, a Venetian blind flanked by foldback shutters, lets in as much light as possible.

Bamboo ladder: Adding a hint of oriental character to the room, the ladder echoes the bamboo edging on the shelves and also serves as a handy towel rail for guests.

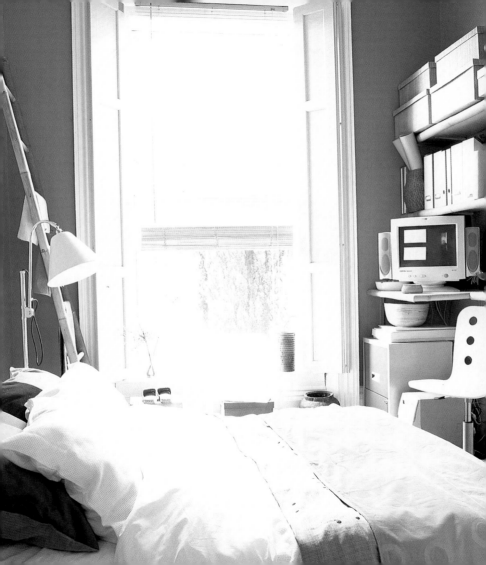

The look: For a modern look with masculine appeal, take your inspiration from the disciplined decor of the orient. Use a monochrome colour scheme to create a smart but calming room environment, or go all the way down the road to Japan by filling your room with furniture and accessories that typify that country's style.

Colour: A monochromatic scheme is based on black, grey and white, although here it is softened slightly by the use of dark blues. Paint the walls in a dark denim shade, applied as a rough colourwash, and add a few Japanese script characters above the bedhead. The natural tones of the paper flooring and wooden furniture add warmth to the scheme.

Bedlinen: Natural cottons and yarn-dyed fabrics are in character here. Keep patterns simple, with smart two-colour checks and stylized oriental prints, and limit your palette to dark blues and pale neutrals. Include some plain white bedlinen to freshen the look, perhaps embroidered with Japanese script.

Furniture: Low-level furniture is the epitome of Japanese style. A futon bed is a must, and an oriental-style screen will both define your theme and do a useful job of concealing clutter to maintain the required standards of minimalism. Look for furniture with clean lines, made of timber with an oiled or varnished finish.

Accessories: Complete the look with paper light shades and a collection of the latest compact audio equipment on your low table. A TV on a turntable makes for easy bedtime viewing. Don't forget to add a money plant for prosperity!

Colour: A deep shade of purple is a bold choice of wall colour which, although it might feel overwhelming if used in a small space, is actually quite a calming shade for a bedroom. If you're aiming for a contemporary scheme, include plenty of white in the room to freshen and lift the overall look. Furnishings in harmonious shades of grey and pink soften the strong contrast between the white and the purple.

Bed: If you can't find a bed with a white frame, choose a budget wooden one and paint it to suit your scheme. A simple design looks best in a contemporary setting – and is also easier to paint.

Bedlinen: Use the bedlinen to introduce texture as well as additional colour into your scheme. Cushions in slubby silks and sheer organza inject a touch of luxury among the plain cotton sheets and pillowcases, while the soft grey blankets and throws add a feeling of comfort.

Storage: Fitted wardrobes are the answer if you need generous storage space in a bedroom. Look for a design that combines hanging rails and shelving so that it can take all types of clothing. Solid wall-to-wall wardrobe doors can look overwhelming in a bedroom, so choosing ones with frosted glass panels is a good idea – if you don't mind glimpsing the contents through them. Another advantage is that glass brightens a room by reflecting light back into it. Frosted glass may be expensive but you can give plain panes a similar look by covering them with glass etch spray, available from DIY or craft stores.

BEDROOM TIP
Plan your clothes storage to suit your personal needs. If you have a lot of long dresses, you'll need hanging space, but if sweaters are more your style you may want a larger number of shelves or drawers

The look: Oriental inspiration is behind the clean lines and minimalist styling of this dramatically modern scheme, which goes all-out for impact with bold blocks of red, pink and white.

Colour: The strong cranberry red of the walls and bedcovers dominates the room to create a cocoon of warmth. Hot colours make a space feel smaller so, to alleviate this effect, bands of lighter pink are painted near ceiling level. Fading the colours from deep red through strong pink to palest pink leads the eye upwards and creates an impression of height. A thin stripe of red separates the two shades. Pure white lightens the mood, contrasting with the cranberry to add graphic impact, while the floorcovering provides a natural base.

Bedlinen: The striking bedlinen gives a modern twist to traditional elements of an English country look – rose prints and gingham. The bold black and red rose motifs and simple checks introduce an element of pattern that highlights the powerful effect of the plain colours.

Furniture: Low-level furniture reinforces the oriental feel of the room. The straight lines and sharp angles of the Japanese bed and modern bedside table enhance the hard-edged modern look, which is softened slightly by the curves of the white chair.

Lighting: Clever lighting varies the mood created by the bold reds. Low-level lamps give a cosy, relaxing glow, while whiter light from overhead adds an invigorating feel. Modern fittings are in tune with the clean lines of the furniture: the square white paper wall light stands out as a starkly simple focal point against the deep red background.

Furniture: An ingenious all-in-one unit solves the storage problem in this small bedroom in a particularly neat way. The specially made MDF structure incorporates a bed base and frame, wardrobes at the head of the bed and, at the base, a desk unit with ample shelf space above.

Office area: The desk part of the MDF unit extends from floor to ceiling at the foot of the bed, successfully dividing the room into two functional spaces – a bedroom and an office – without wasting any space. When the office area is not in use, bamboo blinds can be lowered to conceal the files and other clutter on the shelves.

Walls: In this bold but simple scheme, a rich cream on the walls contrasts with the deep blue used to paint the multi-purpose unit. To link the two colours and add interest to the bed area, narrow blue stripes are painted across the ceiling above it and on the wall at the head of the bed.

Bedlinen: Fabric paint was used to paint stripes onto the cream bedlinen, to make it look as if they are continuing down from the wall. The stripes were masked off, then painted using a narrow roller. The paint, from craft stores, is fixed by ironing the reverse of the fabric. Before painting, slip some scrap fabric or paper inside the pillowcase or duvet cover, to prevent the paint from bleeding through to the other side.

BEDROOM TIP

If you have to use part of your bedroom as a home office, make sure you keep it distinct from your sleeping area by hiding it behind a screen or partition, otherwise you might feel as if you're taking your work to bed with you

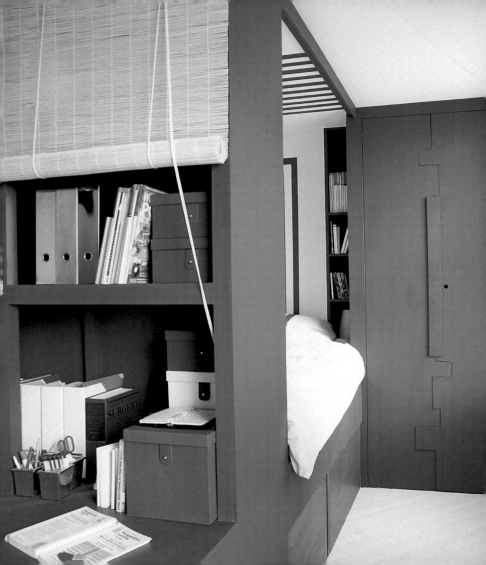

Colour: The fruity shades of the colourful blanket inspired this room's strawberry pink scheme. This strong colour is used all over the walls to make the large room feel warm and cosy. Pale pink curtains and white bedlinen provide a touch of light relief.

Curtains: Several curtain panels are needed to dress the big bay window. Look for cheap fabric and you can afford to be generous with your curtains; full-length drapes look more luxurious than those that end at the windowsill. This pretty pink fabric, an Indian cotton, was picked up for just £2 per metre at a market, so check out your local stalls for bargain buys. A valance at the top adds a decorative heading.

Wardrobe doors: To avoid breaking up the colour on the walls, the doors of the fitted wardrobes are painted in a toning pink, which makes them blend in with the background. When revamping furniture,

don't forget the details – orange glass door knobs are the perfect finishing touch for this scheme.

Radiator: Although none of us would want to be without the heat they produce, radiators often spoil the look of a room. Make them less noticeable by painting them to match your walls. Special radiator paints are available from DIY stores in a range of colours. Alternatively, if they don't include the colour you want, apply a multi-surface primer to the radiator and you can then add a topcoat of any gloss or satinwood paint.

The look: Hot golds and oranges give this room the sun-baked feel of warmer climes. Deep brown wood tones, woven furnishings and layers of lavishly draped coloured fabrics all contribute to the exotic look.

Colour: Warm, vibrant colours will give even the chilliest room a cosy and inviting atmosphere. Sunny golden yellow radiates warmth from the walls, and furnishings in deep glowing shades such as orange and terracotta turn up the heat even further. If you want an exotic feel, base your scheme on the colours of spices – saffron, paprika and ginger. Dark brown furniture ensures that there is a good balance of tones, while fresh white bedlinen lightens up the look to prevent the strong shades from feeling too overpowering.

Furniture: For an ethnic look, focus on natural materials, with furniture made of dark woods and wicker. Low pieces evoke an oriental feel – here a foot-stool works well as a roomy bedside table.

Bedlinen: As for furniture, keep your soft furnishings natural. Plain white cotton serves well as basic bedlinen, then add colour with ethnic-style throws in fine cottons or linens. A woven rush cushion echoes the wicker bedside table, while a fleecy cushion and mohair throw add cosier texture for real warmth during cold northern nights.

Window: To get that lavishly layered effect, team thicker curtains with a sheer panel. Sheers are now available in many different colours, so don't automatically opt for cool white. Here the hot colour continues with a bright orange panel that matches the hessian curtains yet allows ample daylight to filter through.

BEDROOM TIP
If you want to layer drapes at a window, check out your furnishing store for a double curtain pole. This allows you to hang two layers of curtains without resorting to net wire

Colour: For a look that's totally up-to-date, this room sticks with one intense colour that is used throughout in a mixture of different shades, from dark to light. This idea works particularly well with blues, which need only the addition of white to freshen and lift the look. Layer aqua, indigo and turquoise in soft furnishings and wall colours.

Wall stripes: Go to town on tonal variation by painting just one wall in stripes of different shades. Start with the darkest tone at floor level, then paint each successive stripe in a lighter shade until you reach the ceiling. Mask off the first stripe, then paint it and leave to dry before removing the tape and starting on the next one.

Bedlinen: Covers and pillowcases in fresh brilliant white and a brighter shade of turquoise than the moody blues used on the walls ensure that the bed is the focal point of the room. The darker cushion with stripes in a range of tones echoes the wall decoration behind the bed.

Window: The curtains frame the window with the darkest tones of blue and indigo but are sheer enough to keep the overall look light and modern. The tab-top heading suits the contemporary character of the scheme.

Furniture: Modern aluminium and stainless steel furniture will complete the clean, upbeat look. A metal bed frame with simple lines teams up with shiny zinc cupboards to give the scheme an industrial edge.

The look: The stuff of fairy tales – a traditional four-poster decked with flowing white voile set against a dreamy shade of lilac – is given an oriental twist with exotic accessories.

Colour: To highlight fresh white bed drapes, use muted shades for the background: the mid-tone lilac on the walls blends with the pale grey carpet. In a room with a four-poster, painting the ceiling the same shade as the walls maximizes the colour contrast with the drapes, as the top of the bed frame is viewed against it. The purple on the wide skirtings shows a touch of originality, and chimes with the richer colours of the bedhanging.

Bed drapes: Lengths of white voile draped as swags around the top of the four-poster are continued down to the floor at each corner and looped casually around the bed frame. Their ethereal quality is contrasted by the rich, sumptuous colours and gold embroidery of the oriental banner strung across the top of the bed frame. The plain white bedlinen also has a glamorous eastern touch: it is covered with tiny mirrors that sparkle like jewels.

Furniture: The scrolls of the traditional-style iron bed and metal table add to the fanciful feel of the room. The ornate silver chair is oriental in origin.

Accessories: This room shows how accessories can make a powerful statement, as it is they that really define the oriental theme. In addition to the bed banner, Asian art is represented by the hangings and prints on the wall behind the bed, which hail from several different countries.

BOHEMIAN

The look: A touch of old-fashioned romance is added to this bedroom without compromising its contemporary mood. New romantic style goes hand in hand with easy living – instead of fulsome frills and heavy florals, it's kept simple with faded prints and an eclectic mix of furniture.

Colour: Pastel colours score highest for fairytale bedrooms. Pale pinks, blues and greens with plenty of white or cream makes a dreamy mix. Plain walls keep the look modern, while painting the floorboards in cream rather than white gives a more livable look.

Furniture: Curly wrought-iron furniture and pale painted wood is evocative of the romantic mood. An iron bed is a must, but think eclectic when choosing other furniture. This is your chance to trawl through junk shops for irresistible pieces to fall in love with. An old garden table works just as well as a more expensive wrought-iron console – top it with a fancy mirror for laid-back glamour.

Soft furnishings: Steering clear of bright, blowsy prints in favour of faded florals and pale silks gives a gentler touch. The bed is piled with vintage quilts and floral cushions in toning shades – each print contains at least a little of the wall colour to link the different patterns. Long silk curtains spilling onto the floor are trimmed with pink ribbon and secured with a beaded tieback.

Accessories: Glamour comes from sparkly beading and reflective glassware. Go girly with a glass dish full of diamante jewellery and silk flowers, look for beaded lampshades and bags, and keep pretty perfume bottles on display.

BEDROOM TIP
Add definition to pale-coloured curtains by trimming them down the leading edge with brighter ribbon. It also helps to protect delicate fabric from fingermarks or wear and tear each time the curtain is pulled across

Colour: An all-white scheme could easily look cold and clinical in a bedroom; what it needs is a clever touch with texture and pattern to add comfort and interest. In this cosy room, the panel-effect on the wooden bed surround, the soft gathers of the fabric inserts and the luxurious texture of the bedcovering and cushions all spell success for a cool, creamy look.

Bed: An MDF structure built around and above the bed turns it into a magnificent modern four-poster. Rectangles cut out on either side allow access to the small shelves that serve as bedside tables. These 'windows' and the other cutout panels behind and above the bed, which are backed with gathered fabric, help to alleviate the boxy quality of the wood. To add further interest, vertical lines are marked on the bedhead panel to give it the look of tongue-and-groove boards.

Bedlinen: A fake-fur throw adds instant comfort to a bed, as well as texture to a plain colour scheme. The ridged pattern of this one echoes the lines marked on the bedhead. Piling the bed with cushions and pillows gives a totally sumptuous feel and offers the opportunity to add further, but more subtle, texture with delicate white lace edgings and figured patterns.

Accessories: The symmetry of the scheme is emphasized by a pair of wood and canvas chairs placed beneath mirrors on either side of the bed. The child's portrait, an eye-catching focal point at the centre of the bedhead, adds a personal touch that gives the room a more homely feel.

Colour: Blues form the basic palette of this contemporary scheme, with the icy shade on the walls punctuated with a brighter border above the navy headboard. With a carpet in a pale neutral, most of the vibrant colour comes from the bedlinen, particularly the two quilts in turquoise and candy pink. The striped lampshade and brocade cushion add accents of hotter pink.

Walls: Wood panelling gives walls an elegant look – try creating mock panels by gluing on strips of moulding from DIY stores. Panels also offer the chance to be creative with colour – the border of bright blue and the paisley motifs stamped in the same shade make a feature of the wall behind the bed.

Bedlinen: Layers of sumptuous fabrics and beautiful embroidery add an air of luxury to the light, pretty colour scheme. The two bedspreads are made of silk satin, their quilted lines adding both pattern and texture. Their bright colours are balanced by cushions and pillowcases in pastel shades, made of velvet, silk and cotton and embroidered with flowers and butterflies.

Furniture: Although the furniture is all contemporary in style, a mix of different materials gives an eclectic look. The bed has a fabric-covered headboard, the chair is wood and rattan and the nest of bedside tables is clear Perspex, wonderful for enhancing the feeling of light and space.

Mirror: A full-length mirror is a useful addition to a bedroom or dressing area. A freestanding model is more versatile than one fixed to a door, so make a feature of it by choosing a design that suits your scheme.

The look: Using hot shades of pink throughout a bedroom creates a look brimming with warmth and passion. This scheme combines its exotic burst of colour with oriental influences, such as the bamboo bedside table and the sari fabrics used to make some of the soft furnishings.

Colour: One guaranteed way of making a striking colour statement is to use the same vibrant shade for the walls, carpet and bedspread – just make sure you love the colour first! Accents of deep purple, which is a calming colour, add a hint of spirituality to offset the passionate quality of the hot pink, while flashes of white freshen the mood.

Furniture: Its black frame gives the bed a strong presence against the brightly coloured backdrop, and echoes the dark tones of the purple furnishings. For an oriental feel, add rustic furniture made of natural eastern materials, such as this wooden bedside cabinet with bamboo-panelled door. Pieces made from wicker, rattan and bamboo are usually great value for money, and reasonably priced Asian imports are now widely available from high-street stores. Check out mail-order companies too.

Soft furnishings: Choose shiny, silky fabrics for oriental boudoir-style glamour. Saris are ideal – they are long enough to make colourful sheer curtains and can be cut up to cover cushions. Look for saris that have gold borders or embroidery that you can incorporate in your makes to add glitzy decorative detail.

Accessories: Keep the oriental theme going with Japanese-style prints, ornately embroidered or beaded bags and brightly coloured candles and vases with bold, simple shapes.

The look: In this neat contemporary scheme, a number of creative storage solutions keep clutter under control at the same time as adding style and shape. Pretty pinks and rose prints add a tender touch.

Colour: The pink on the walls gives a warm, mid-tone background that shows off to advantage the white storage furniture and bedlinen. The subtle rose design on the duvet cover and pillowcases pretties things up without overdoing the floweriness, while the red valance keeps the overall look smart by underlining the bed with punchy colour.

Storage: Look for storage features that do their job but are also designed to be seen. Here the space-age curves of the bedside table and the plastic hanging unit add cutting-edge style to the room. The larger shelving unit has a sheer fabric cover that can be lowered to give a neat look but is also transparent enough to show off the stylish storage boxes inside. Be imaginative with space to store items you don't need on a daily basis; out-of-season clothes can be stashed away in wooden boxes on castors that slot neatly under the bed.

Valance: A valance doesn't have to be all frills and flounces: get practical and sew yourself a simple modern design with pockets on the outside – they make great hidey-holes for pairs of shoes. The valance also does an effective job of concealing any boxes or bags stored underneath the bed.

BEDROOM TIP
Small storage boxes are ideal for keeping dressing tables and other surfaces clear of jewellery and cosmetics. If you want to keep the contents within easy reach, invest in beautiful boxes that you'll be proud to show off

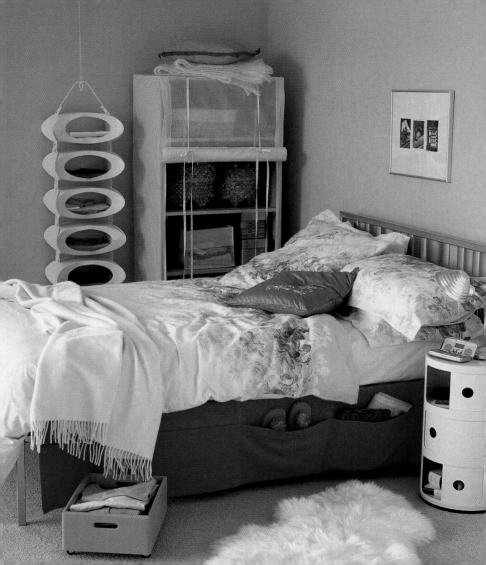

The look: Rough wooden flooring and an industrial-style metal bed frame create an interesting contrast with prettily patterned bedlinen. The look is one of contemporary chic which appears casual but relies for its success on careful pattern mixing.

Colour: Cool contemporary lilac will add a sophisticated note to the most spartan of rooms. Used on the walls, a muted mid-tone provides a quiet backdrop for a mix of patterns in similar shades and toning colours. The bold coloured stripes of the curtains reflect both the natural tones of the floorboards and the blue accent provided by the chair.

Pattern: A bed offers lots of scope for mixing patterns, so be creative with cushions, covers and pillowcases. Set the scene with one key colour, then make sure most of the patterns contain that shade. The starting point here is the strong lilac stripe on the duvet cover. For an interesting eclectic look, mix prints in several different fabrics, from chintz to Indian silks. Try to achieve a balance between small spriggy prints and larger or bolder designs.

Papered panel: While plain walls are best for showing off a mixture of prints, an element of pattern adds interest to an unadorned corner. Create a movable feature by covering a tall panel of MDF with a subtly patterned wallpaper in a colour that tones with the walls.

Accessories: The shiny vase and lampbase reflect the silvery quality of the lilac furnishings and the metal bed. The red shade and flowers add bright accents to intensify the muted colours in the room.

The look: Just made for the city slicker, this room combines a contemporary colour scheme in smart neutrals with seductive leather and suede to create a cosy love nest.

Colour: Plain white walls and pale wood flooring put the emphasis on the furnishings. The high black headboard looks important against the white walls, marking out the bed as the focal point. The tan cushions and throw cosy up the look with a warmer colour, although without straying from the neutral theme.

Bed: Tactile leather and suede have a playboy image that's ideal for this room. Get their expensive looks for less by using cheaper lookalikes. Leatherette covers both the base of the divan and the impressively large headboard, made by covering MDF with thick wadding, then stapling the leatherette in place at the back. Cushions covered in artificial suede join with the huge fake fur throw to add further sensuous texture to the bed, while crisp white linen keeps the look smart.

Accessories: The modern art on the wall is a DIY version of Jackson Pollock's splatter-painted masterpieces. Dilute emulsion colours with one part water to three parts paint, then dip a brush in the paint and splatter over ready-stretched canvases. Make sure you cover the surrounding area with plenty of newspaper!

Floor: The plywood floor has been given a tiled effect. Mark out 60cm squares, then simply colour in the lines with a thick black marker pen to resemble tiles. Seal the surface with a few coats of matt varnish.

The look: Oriental style has two faces: it can be either cleanly minimalist or sumptuously sensual. Use its more exotic elements to make a boudoir of your bedroom by letting rip with hot colours, sheeny silks and layers of beautifully embroidered bedlinen.

Colour: Think opulent for your colour scheme, with rich, rosy pinks and deep, sultry purples. If you would rather use a pale shade on the walls, see that the bed provides plenty of colour power with vibrant coverings and cushions. Keeping the flooring natural will help to calm down the colour fest, but choose warm neutrals and textured rugs for maximum comfort.

Walls: Delicate cherry blossom or orchid designs will spell out the style. Here flower stencils have been used to decorate the panelled wall, the motifs applied with stencil paints using subtle shades of grey and violet. Don't overdo the floral decoration – just a few delicate designs will do the trick.

Bedlinen: The embroidered flowers on the white cotton sheets and pillowcases echo the cherry blossom motifs on the walls. Other coverings and cushions introduce the luxurious oriental silks and brocades that are so important to this style. Details such as glamorous beading, Chinese-style rouleau fastenings and the chunky knots on the purple quilt also add character.

Furniture: Complete the look with rustic furniture and accessories that form a striking contrast with the opulent furnishings. Bamboo furniture not only scores points for oriental style but will also be kind to your purse. Simple paper light shades and plain ceramic vases fit the bill as finishing touches.

BEDROOM TIP
Floral furnishings and decorations create a look, but fresh flowers and plants can really bring it to life. Display potted orchids or sprays of blossom to enhance an oriental theme, colourful spring blooms for a country-style room or lush green foliage for a colonial style

The look: The natural look turns soft in this room, with its focus on knitted throws and cushions in warm wool and jersey. With a dose of hot pink to take the chill out of the neutral and white colour scheme, the scene is set for serious snuggling up.

Colour: The colour scheme reflects the emphasis on natural fabrics by using mostly neutral shades. White walls and bedlinen create a plain backdrop to show off the textured furnishings. The linen curtain and many of the knits themselves are also in natural shades, to keep the overall look simple and contemporary in style. The vibrant pinks and reds of the striped throw form a strong contrast and draw the eye to the bed, their burst of bold, warm colour giving it a more inviting look.

Bedcoverings: The comfy furnishings that form the centrepiece of this snuggly scheme comprise a selection of different knits – from fine jersey to thick wool – as well as soft fleecy fabrics. If you're nifty with a pair of needles, have a go at knitting your own cushions and throws – use chunky wool and big needles and they'll grow quickly.

Curtain: Underlining the theme of the room, a knitted scarf makes an original tieback for the single linen curtain panel, which is draped right across the window in a decorative fashion.

Furniture: Wooden furniture suits the natural scheme, and its blond colour enhances the light, contemporary look. The blanket box makes a good window seat, as well as providing useful storage space.

BEDROOM TIP
If you have some old woollen jumpers you no longer want, cut them up to make cushion covers. To prevent the knitting unravelling, machine a zigzag stitch close to each cut edge before sewing the pieces together

The look: Revving up the passion creates your own sumptuous love den with layers of luxurious fabrics and opulent shades of pink and purple. A deep-pile carpet and touchy-feely textures combine to indulge the senses.

Colour: Deep pink equals passion, and when used to cover the walls gives a room an all-round feeling of warmth. To create a moody air, use a muted rather than a bright tone. Purple enriches the look, while dull pewters and smoky greys set the seal on the sultry atmosphere. Don't weaken the look with too much white – include a glimpse to heighten the effect of the deeper colours. The pale grey carpet also helps to highlight the darker tones used on the bed.

Bed: Pile the bed with duvets, cushions and throws in a variety of sensuous textures, from cosy lambswool to flamboyant fake fur. If you can't afford silk sheets and pillowcases, choose finely embroidered white cotton, then splash out on more luxurious fabrics in smaller quantities for the cushion covers. Mix slubby silks and smooth satins with plush velvets and a touch of grey lace. A headboard covered in suede-effect fabric adds to the feeling of opulence and gives greater emphasis to the bed.

Carpet: Choose a carpet that really pampers bare feet, such as a soft shag-pile. For ultimate luxury, top it with a toe-tickling furry rug or two.

Furniture: Wrought-iron furniture and a Gothic-style candelabra add to the dramatic romance of the scheme, while a stylish chair upholstered in purple velvet enhances the feeling of comfort.

BEDROOM TIP
Candles set the mood for romance. Turn your bedroom into a real pleasure zone by burning scented or aromatherapy candles – but remember to blow them out before you go to sleep

Colour: If you want a light background to increase the illusion of space in a room but also like bold colours, try a compromise solution. Dashes of hot raspberry pink counter-act the iciness of the pale blue walls and the white woodwork, ceiling and duvet cover. Used in panels on the bed canopy, they create a striking focal point in this welcoming contemporary scheme.

Bed canopy: A canopy makes a dramatic decorative feature, especially in a high-ceilinged bedroom. With none of the floaty fussiness of traditional four-poster drapes, this simple design uses colourful stripes to make a bold modern state-ment. It is made by sewing together strips of pink and white muslin into a canopy the width of the bed, then draping this over two pieces of dowelling fixed to the ceiling with cup hooks. The padded headboard is covered with thicker fabrics in bands of matching colour.

Cushions: Cushions are an excellent way of adding small amounts of colour and pattern to a bedroom. Pretty 1950s florals and natural linens soften the contrast between the hot pink stripes and the snow white bedlinen, while the bright blue cushion punctuates the scheme with another bold colour. Use trimmings to add extra interest to plain cushions – floral braid and coloured ribbon can easily be sewn onto covers.

Blinds: To avoid distracting attention from the bed, the small windows are dressed in ultra-simple fashion, with canvas Roman blinds in a pale cream which melts into the light background.

BEDROOM TIP
Use runners to cover worn surfaces, protect polished furniture from wear and stains or simply to add a splash of colour. Cut a strip of fabric long enough to cover your chest of drawers or table, and then hem the edges

The look: The decorative period-style dressing table and mirror form the focal point of this room. With their delicate curvy shapes, pale colouring and elaborate golden embellishments in the form of bows, flowers and leaves, they set the tone for a look of ornate elegance that has a very feminine feel.

Colour: The cream paint on the walls tones with the colour of the dressing table and mirror, but it provides a plain enough backdrop to put the furniture in the limelight and show up the intricacies of its decorative details. The light, neutral look continues with the carpet, in a pale shade of taupe. The white background of the duvet cover adds a crisp touch to the scheme, and also helps to enhance the richness of the cream walls. Its sprays of coloured blooms add floral charm to the bed, to balance the prettiness of the ornate furniture.

Furniture: The dressing table, stool and mirror are 1950s pieces made in Rococo style. The chair near the wardrobe, with its gleaming scrolls and velvet padding, echoes the elaborate elegance and gold detailing of the other furniture. Reflected in the mirror is a large, ornate candelabra, which fits in well with the theatrical feel of the room. The bed is painted in pale pink, a colour picked out from the floral design of the bedlinen.

Wardrobe doors: Panelled detailing adds interest and a hint of classical style to the floor-to-ceiling fitted wardrobes. Painting the doors in the same colour as the walls makes them fade into the background without imposing on the scheme and stealing attention from the furniture.

The look: Fresh lime-green walls add a shot of contemporary colour to this colonial-style room, where mosquito netting, ethnically patterned bedlinen and exotic accessories all convey the idea of comfort in a hot climate.

Colour: Colonial colour schemes are traditionally based on neutral shades, complemented by plenty of natural materials such as wood and wicker. The natural tones of the bedlinen adhere to this tradition but the lime-green walls update the look. As a colour of nature, green goes well with wooden furnishings, but choosing a fresh lime shade sharpens up the overall scheme, giving it a refreshing contemporary edge.

Bed: A colonial-style bedroom demands a mosquito netting bed canopy. Nets are widely available from travel shops for a few pounds, and come ready to hang – simply fix hooks into your ceiling and then drape the netting around the head of your bed. Cotton bedcovers with ethnic prints reinforce the theme further, while a couple of silky yellow cushions provide a touch of luxury.

Window: To keep things natural, leave the window frames and other woodwork unpainted and fit a wooden Venetian blind to provide privacy. To give the window a more romantic look, team this with sheer white curtains, softly draped to echo the bed canopy. The tab-top heading of these curtains enhances the room's contemporary feel.

Accessories: A scheme like this makes a good showcase for decorative souvenirs brought back from exotic holidays. If you haven't travelled that far, see what local shops have to offer in the way of foreign imports. Family photographs and potted foliage plants also help to create the look.

The look: This cosy bedroom is in a converted loft, but the character of the scheme gives the impression of an undisturbed attic, still with its unfinished ceiling, open beams and clutter of forgotten books and suitcases. The lack of proper furniture suggests a casual, makeshift feel with a certain element of romance, as if the owners have discovered their own secret corner of the house to camp out in.

Colour: The dull colours of the bedding reflect the fusty feel of the attic, with shades of dusty grey, faded purple and tarnished gold. The white pillows, nestling under the lowest point of the roof, add a light touch against the cosy darkness of the brown sloping ceiling and rough wooden beams.

Bed: The bed has no base, consisting simply of a mattress covered with blue and white striped fabric, with bedlinen laid on top. The cotton mattress cover and pillows keep things simple, while throws in more sumptuous fabrics add a hint of glamour: the gold one has a silky sheen, while the grey cover is edged with a border of purple crushed velvet. The cushion adds an element of pattern, with an appropriately traditional design in golds and browns.

Accessories: The battered suitcase adds character and serves as storage, and the pile of old books beside the bed makes a handy perch for the alarm clock. Candles enhance the romantic setting, while a modern lamp lifts the gloom with brighter light if required.

The look: The exotic scheme for this tiny guest bedroom is based on a Bedouin tent. The look is created with billowing muslin drapes, a bright orange colourwash on the walls and richly patterned furnishings.

Walls: Hot, vivid colour is essential for a Moroccan-style room. Earthy reds, golds and terracottas all work well, but as warm colours tend to make a room feel smaller, it's best to use a bright rather than a deep shade in a room this tiny. Applying this sunny orange as a wash creates a rough, broken effect that suits the rustic style of the room.

Ceiling drapes: White muslin is inexpensive to buy, so you won't break the bank by using it in the abundance required by this scheme. To get the tented ceiling effect, hang copper rods from your ceiling by fixing cup hooks at each end, then drape many metres of muslin over the top of them. Continue the fabric down to floor level at either side of the window to make sheer curtains, tying them about a third of the way down in a loose knot for a decorative tied-back effect.

Sofa bed: A simple sofa bed that converts into a low seat is ideal for this look, and its patterned upholstery includes deep blues, reds and yellows suggestive of Moorish style.

Accessories: Add a Moroccan rug as a wallhanging, a couple of cushions trimmed with tassels, and a few pieces of blue and white pottery to really define the look. Candles bring a romantic glow to desert nights – look for decorative metal or pottery holders.

The look: An extravagantly dressed four-poster and an arresting colour scheme are the key ingredients of this highly theatrical look. Sharp citrus green covers the ceiling as well as the walls, so that anyone looking up towards the top of the four-poster gets the full effect of its contrast with the striking scarlet bed drapes. The swathes of red velvet and the ornate period-style furniture give the room a luxuriously decadent feel.

Bed: The magnificent bed, with its beautifully carved wooden posts and lavish drapes, is undeniably the focal point, but setting it at an angle gives it even greater presence and emphasizes the individualistic style of the room. Stunning fabric effects don't always require sewing skill – lengths of red velvet have simply been wound around the top of the bed frame and then draped down behind the wooden headboard.

Fireplace: If an original fireplace has been removed, just painting the remaining alcove in a contrasting colour can transform it into an eye-catching feature. A dramatic floral display softens the boxiness of the space.

Flooring: Natural flooring forms a calming base for the flamboyant furnishings. Choose a tone that's strong enough to match your wall colour but not so dark that it's in danger of dominating the scheme. This warm beige offsets the acid sharpness of the green and tones with the richly coloured wood of the furniture.

Accessories: Glamorous or offbeat accessories, such as the red silk lampshades, mirror and wire dress dummy, add to the decadent feel of the room.

The look: The country cottage look has enduring appeal, especially for bedrooms, and here it has been updated for the 21st century, still with delicate floral prints and timber furniture but without finicky frills and flounces.

Floral prints: A mix of floral prints is essential to this style, and they are blended in fabrics and wallpapers. To keep the look contemporary, a wallpaper with an understated design was used – small spriggy buds or flowers in subtle colours rather than bright blowsy blooms. The bed is layered with traditional quilts and old-fashioned florals, but their busy look is balanced with plenty of plain fabrics in sheets and pillowcases.

Colour: A restricted colour palette means that you can successfully mix as many patterned fabrics as take your fancy. Here soft pinks and blues have been used throughout the room, and all the prints feature one or both of these colours.

Furniture: Wooden furniture is a must for a country-style room, but a modern interpretation of the look calls for pieces with cleaner, more contemporary lines. They don't have to be brand new, just simple in style. The same goes for wooden accessories, such as picture frames.

Window: Fussy frills and girly gathers are banished in favour of sleek, pared-down window treatments. This simple roll-up blind teams a subtle floral on the window side with a plain pink that helps to calm down the mix of patterns in the room. Satin ribbons in blue, the other key colour of the scheme, act as tie-ups, their bows adding a pretty finishing touch that's perfect for the look.

Colour: If you're a lover of pink, the bedroom is a great place to experiment with colour. Sugary pinks bring a bright, modern feel to this attic room. Warmer than pastel pinks but more refreshing than deeper shades, the candy colour used on the walls creates a stimulating atmosphere. The much lighter tone on the sloping ceiling adds a feeling of space and height to the room, and echoes the pale pink bedspread. The chair and striped blind add accents of green that sharpen the look.

Bed: The floral bedspread joins with the cushion cover on the chair to add subtle pattern to the scheme. The floral and toile de Jouy designs are traditional in style yet not too fussy, so they add just a hint of country charm to bring out the character of the attic setting. Likewise, the half-flower design of the bed frame is simple but decorative, and its brass finish goes well with the warm colours in the room.

Blind: If you want to avoid shutting out natural light during the day, but need something more substantial than a sheer curtain to provide privacy in the evening, a Roman blind makes a practical window treatment. It's easy to make one using a kit, available from haberdashery stores. The kit includes fixtures, fittings and instructions – everything except the fabric and battens. Stripes work well as Roman blinds because their design complements the straight lines of the pleats.

Carpet: A natural-coloured carpet provides a calming neutral base for the vibrant pink. Choose a mid-tone such as camel or beige rather than a paler shade, to enhance the warm feeling created by the wall colour.

Colour: Light-as-a-whisper pinks and blues, the colours of delicate spring blossom, create a deliriously feminine bedroom. A pastel combination steers clear of sugariness if you keep the shades airily pale, while subtle floral designs used in strict moderation add prettiness without looking too fussy and dated.

Furniture: Only a white bed frame would be light enough to look at home in this room, and delicate curves fit the theme too. The elegant bench at the end of the bed also has a white finish, but including the odd piece of natural wood furniture helps to add warmth to the scheme.

Walls: Many bedrooms stick to plain walls and make patterned bedlinen the focal point, but this scheme takes an alternative approach. A subtle trellis-design paper adds interest to the high walls and introduces floral charm that enhances the feminine feel of the room, yet is understated enough not to dominate the scheme. The lower part of the walls is covered in tongue-and-groove panelling, which bridges the gap between traditional and modern styles. It is painted in a pale blue picked out from the flowers on the wallpaper.

Bedlinen: With patterned walls, the bedlinen is kept plain in colour, although the crisscross design and ridged borders of the blue quilt add textural pattern. The lack of cushions and layered coverings gives a neat look, with extra blankets stacked tidily on the bench.

Window: For such a light, airy look, a sheer curtain is the essential window dressing. This white voile is hung as a simple ungathered panel from a slender pole so as to show off its embroidered floral design.

The look: This room shows how just a few old-fashioned accessories can inject character into a room and form a fascinating focal point in an otherwise plain scheme. The collection of decorative mirrors creates a feeling of faded elegance, which is enhanced by the muted tone used on the walls behind them and by the delicate floral designs of the bedlinen.

Mirrors: Raid junk shops for old mirrors and group them on one wall to make an original feature. The more mismatched the better – include one or two brand-new mirrors and a couple of highly decorative frames in gilt finishes, and the mix will create a look that's high on romance. Tarnished or spotted glass simply adds to the feeling of faded beauty.

Colour: A pale, muted lilac makes a gentle backdrop for the mirrors. The other walls and the flooring (reflected in one of the mirrors) are decorated entirely in clean white, off-setting the worn, aged feel with an atmosphere of space and light. The mirrors also do their bit in reflecting light.

Bedlinen: The colours of the bedlinen echo the two contrasting aspects of the decor by combining clean white and fresh aqua with more muted tones. Small floral designs, quilted covers and embroidered pillowcases and cushions add to the chintzy, old-fashioned feel created by the mirrors.

Chair: The modern metal chair highlights the old versus new theme, contrasting its simple, functional lines with the fanciful mirror frames and punctuating this end of the room with a dose of deeper, more contemporary lilac.

BEDROOM TIP
As well as serving as decorative features and essential dressing aids, mirrors also play a less obvious role in a room scheme. They are invaluable for reflecting light, and can increase the illusion of space in a small room

Colour: With its low sloping ceiling and small window, this loft bedroom is starved of natural light, but a barely-there scheme provides a colour cure. The walls and ceiling are painted in two shades of cream, and white and cream bedlinen enhances the bright, airy effect. Even the dark wood beams have been lightened to alleviate their heavy, gloomy character. Only the wood of the small window frame and the muted browns of the throw and velvet cushion punctuate the scheme with darker accents. The result is a bedroom that retains its country charm, but is instilled with a brighter, more contemporary feel.

Beams: The beams have been lightened by washing their dark wood with diluted white emulsion and then, when dry, rubbing back the paint with sandpaper. This has the effect of revealing the wood grain beneath, so preserving the natural feel of the beams.

Furniture: Keeping the look light, the metal bed has a white finish. Like the beams, the honey-coloured pine of the two bedside cabinets has been toned down, this time by applying a white woodwash.

Blind: A tiny window needs a simple dressing, such as this Roman blind. Like stripes, checked fabric works well with this style of blind. The yellow and tan checks add a hint of colour to the room while toning with the walls.

Accessories: Bedside lamps with simple lines and cream-coloured shades fit in with the room's colour scheme and its pared-down, contemporary feel. The Shaker-style boxes on the sill add a further touch of country style.

The look: Wood tones predominate in this room, where the pine floorboards and furniture set the scene for a country farmhouse feel. They are complemented by a relaxed blue and green colour scheme, an original period fireplace and shapely traditional-style wrought-iron accessories.

Colour: Blue and green is a harmonious colour combination that is sure to create a tranquil atmosphere. Here gentle sea shades suit the natural feel of the room, the walls teaming two light muted tones above and below dado level, and the fireplace tiles featuring a mix of soft jades. The radiator is painted to match the wall and becomes all but invisible.

Curtains: Framing the window, the curtains are a focal point, their vibrant turquoise making them stand out against the more subtle shades of the walls. Over-long, they form lavish pools of fabric on the floor which, along with the big tassel tiebacks used deliberately high, lends them dramatic impact.

Furniture: Made from pine that matches the floorboards, the bed was commissioned from a local craftsman. The chest of drawers is also made of pine, while the wicker laundry basket adds texture to the scheme. The fire surround was found in a salvage yard, a good place to look if you want to replace period features that are beyond repair or have been ripped out by previous owners.

Accessories: Metal accessories with fancy scrolls and spirals, such as the curtain pole, towel rail and tall candlestick, add to the room's traditional character and also echo the black iron of the fireplace.

The look: Flowers spell romance, but this room is modern rather than chintzy in character. Although the bed is layered with a patchwork of prints, they have a crisply coordinated feel, and there is plenty of plain white to offset the cottage-garden effect that a jumble of patterns can create.

Pattern: Red roses run as a theme throughout the bedlinen, where they are repeated in prints of different sizes. The overall colour palette is simple, limited to red, white and lilac, with additional shades appearing only in small details such as leaves. It is the common elements of colour and motif that give the combination of patterns a more organized and contemporary feel than a mix of diverse florals ever could.

Colour: Pale pinks and lilacs are classic choices as backgrounds for floral prints, but using a deeper shade on the walls creates a bolder, more modern look. This strong lilac provides a striking contrast for the abundance of white used throughout the room, while also toning with the rich red of the rose patterns.

Window: A super-sheer curtain panel keeps the look light, its scattering of delicate blooms adding further floral romance to the room. There are now many modern designs available in patterned sheers – and they have nothing in common with dreary old nets.

Accessories: For a contemporary feel, steer clear of fussy, over-flowery accessories. Look instead for lampshades and pictures with clean lines and modern shapes that feature simple flower motifs in just one or two of the key colours of your scheme.

BEDROOM TIP
It's easy to decorate plain paper lampshades with your own designs. Choose simple motifs that suit your scheme, and use water-based paints applied with a fine artist's paintbrush

The look: Suave and sophisticated, this look derives its character from the luxurious textures of leather and suede, using them for furniture, accessories and bedlinen. A colour scheme of soft lilacs and smoky greys adds to the subtly seductive feel.

Colour: Leather and suede look best in soft, natural shades such as browns and greys. In this room, toning shades of smoky grey melt against the pale lilac walls, while accents of black and white smarten up the scheme to create a comfortable look with a masculine feel.

Leather: Suede and leather can look just as much at home in the bedroom as in the living room. A leather chest is used as a bedside table, and teamed with suede-covered accessories such as the lampbase. If you can't afford real suede cushions, make covers using a lookalike fabric – there are a number of good imitation suedes available from fabric stores.

Headboard: To add to the decadent feel, make a big padded headboard for your bed and cover it with fake suede. Construct a simple MDF box the size you want, pad it with foam or wadding, and then stretch suede-look fabric over the top, fixing it in place at the back of the headboard with a staple gun or tacks.

Walls: The wooden tongue-and-groove panelling on the walls adds an air of country comfort. This may appear to be at odds with the room's decadent feel but it has the effect of relaxing the look at the same time as bringing out the handcrafted, wholesome character of the heavily stitched leather.

The look: Vintage chic meets elements of country style, with a chandelier and display of old plates sharing room space with a patchwork quilt and a floral blind. When set against a cool, contemporary backdrop of plain pale colour, these individual touches come together to create an atmosphere of modern romance.

Colour: Space-enhancing blue covers the walls up to the picture rail, with the white above increasing the illusion of height. The floorboards are also painted white for an especially bright and airy effect. Lines of flower motifs stencilled in a subtle shade of grey add just a hint of romance to the walls.

Soft furnishings: While many a country-style room would have a bed piled high with quilts and floral prints, this scheme keeps patterned furnishings to a minimum, with the focus falling on a single patchwork cover highlighted against plain white bedlinen. A few silky cushions pick out pastel colours from the quilt. The only block of floral fabric is the rose print at the window, which is made up in a clean-cut style – a Roman blind – that shows off its design to best effect.

Furniture: The eclectic mix of furniture reflects the diverse influences behind the scheme. A few well-chosen pieces with character will suit a relaxed style, but beware of crowding out the room with furniture if you want to retain an uncluttered contemporary feel.

Accessories: If you have a collection to display, make a feature of it by building a purpose-made shelf system. Together with the chandelier, the decorative plates add a classic feel to the room.

The look: Inspired by the clean, cool style of New England homes, this scheme offsets a subtle lilac wall colour with fresh white on the woodwork and ceiling. Both shades work well with the warm wood tones of the sanded floorboards.

Bedlinen: Soft furnishings often take centre stage in a bedroom, and here a mix of textures and patterns focuses attention on the bed. Simple narrow stripes and small gingham-style checks create an air of country-style comfort, but monochrome colours – black, grey and navy – give the look a smarter modern edge. There is just the occasional floral print to vary the pace. A valance made of white waffle-weave fabric conceals the base of the divan.

Curtains: Softly gathered cream curtains in a linen and cotton mix cover the large expanse of window, their pale colour enhancing the light, airy quality of the room. They are trimmed with vertical borders of grey velvet ribbon, which gives them definition and links them with the other colours in the room.

Furniture: The honey-coloured rattan chair and bedside table echo the wooden tones of the flooring, while the white chest of drawers complements the woodwork. White furniture creates a clean, modern-country feel, so try bringing old pine chests up to date with a coat of paint.

Accessories: A relaxed scheme like this allows for an eclectic selection of accessories: an abstract modern mirror sits comfortably alongside a checked country-style bag and a jug of fresh garden flowers.

The look: With its wood-panelled walls, lacy bedlinen and old-fashioned accessories, this bedroom's look is classic country – with its roots in manor house elegance rather than cottage chintz. The colour scheme of muted turquoise and lilac was suggested by the flower prints on the wall.

Walls: The walls are covered entirely with wood panelling, to re-create the look of an old country house. Tongue-and-groove planks are widely available from DIY stores and timber merchants, and can be cut to size and fixed in place by anyone who's competent at DIY. They can then be painted – gloss and satinwood give wood a hard-wearing sheen, while emulsion has a less durable matt finish. The wall behind the bed is painted in two tones of turquoise, a panel of the darker shade forming a frame effect that makes a focal point of the large gilt-framed picture.

Alcove: Highlighted in lilac, the alcove beside the bed makes a perfect display space for a few framed photographs and a pot plant. When switched on, the spotlight at the top turns it into an eye-catching feature of the room, and focuses the attention on its contents.

Soft furnishings: Classic white bedlinen with delicate lace trim evokes a traditional feel, and its lightness of colour and texture forms a fresh contrast with the moody tones of the wood panelling. The window is also dressed in white, with a simple, lightly gathered sheer curtain.

Accessories: Old prints and period-style ornaments follow through the classic character of the room. The brackets of the shelves have a gilt finish to match the frame above the bed.

The look: In this unashamedly feminine bedroom that's full of cottage-garden charm, a profusion of floral prints in pretty pinks runs riot. To give the look a contemporary feel, whitewashed wood and sheer curtains keep things fresh.

Floral prints: A number of floral prints are mixed successfully by choosing one key colour – in this case pink – and making sure they all contain that shade. Vary the size of the designs, combining small spriggy buds with big bold blooms, and look for fabrics that feature plenty of white to give a clean feel.

Colour: Pink is a popular choice for a scheme based on pretty florals. Using a plain mid-tone on the walls highlights the fresh white background and busy patterns of the prints. Using a stronger tone – as in the pink chair – adds depth to a predominantly light look.

Furniture: Traditional styling and elegant curves complement the old-fashioned appeal of the floral fabrics. Iron beds are available in a wide range of designs. In order to keep the overall look light, a white bed frame was chosen and teamed with white-painted wooden furniture with an aged finish – a console table with drawers does the job of a dressing table. An upholstered armchair adds a touch of comfort.

Curtains: Hanging sheer fabric at the windows continues the airy look. Don't try to be too coordinated – the curtains don't have to match the bedlinen exactly – but if you choose a different print, make sure that it works with those on the bed.

BEDROOM TIP
Think how the colours you choose will affect the mood of your room. In a bedroom, paler pink will create a reassuring, restful atmosphere, whereas a shocking shade or a stimulating scarlet will have a far more rousing effect

The look: Colour is used to create a striking look on a budget by making the best of basic or worn wooden furniture with a bold, bright backdrop.

Colour: A vibrant, no-holds-barred cerise adorns the window wall of this bedroom, with the radiators painted to match. However, the sloping ceiling is painted in light pink to avoid overwhelming the room with strong colour. The bedlinen also lightens the look, with understated shades of pink and cream, while the gold curtains add a second warm, glowing colour to the mix.

Walls: Bold as the cerise looks, it has in fact been toned down from the original shade. Stir a small amount of cream emulsion into pink paint, and then dilute the mixture with water. The result is a colourwashed effect, which not only gives strong pink a softer, more livable look, but also economizes on paint as it makes a little go a long way.

Furniture: The rough wooden finish of the huge wardrobe and the bedhead gives the room a natural, rustic feel. The rattan laundry basket, which doubles as a casual bedside table, is also in tune with this mood.

Curtains: Markets and junk shops can be excellent cheap sources of curtain material – the fabric for these cost just £2. If you find a bargain fabric, you can afford to go for quantity rather than quality, so be generous with the amount you buy. A cheap fabric used in full-length drapes with lavish gathers can look more effective than an expensive print made up in a skimpier design.

The look: Cosy and lived-in, this is a bedroom where you can really relax. Furniture that's slightly worn at the edges, layers of floral bedlinen and rosy pink walls all put comfort at the top of the agenda.

Colour: To give the whole room a feeling of warmth, the walls are decorated with a mid-toned pink. Soft furnishings in light beiges and creams add just enough white to offset them without freshening the effect too much. A boldly striped rug introduces accents of more vigorous pink which bring the look up to date.

Bedlinen: For snuggly style, the bed is piled with soft, faded linens, then heaped with a huge floral quilt. Scour the shops or make your own from fabric remnants, but remember, the more blooms the merrier!

Headboard: The bed is given a cosier feel with a padded headboard. Cover your existing bedhead or a piece of MDF with foam or wadding, then with fabric that matches your bedlinen or curtains. Use a staple gun to fix it in place at the back of the board.

Furniture: Country-style French furniture adds oodles of character. If you aren't lucky enough to own the real thing, track down a convincing new lookalike. A big pine wardrobe is a must. Wicker and rattan also suit the lived-in look, while curvy white-painted console tables add an air of faded grandeur. If they are old, or have a distressed finish, so much the better.

BEDROOM TIP
If your wardrobe lacks character, cut panels out of the doors and replace them with floral fabric or chicken wire. Hang the fabric from curtain wire fixed behind the door at the top and bottom of each panel. Chicken wire can be secured using a staple gun

Colour: Clear contemporary blues bring a meadow-fresh feel to this room. Include enough different shades of blue in your scheme and it will work without any other colours, except perhaps a few dashes of white as a light contrast.

Pattern: A mixture of smart checks and stripes, all in blue, creates a lively, modern feel. When using different checked fabrics side by side, mix designs in varying sizes, from big bold squares to ginghams. A floral print used in a small way will soften the look slightly – here a subtle sprigged wallpaper makes a feature of an odd-shaped corner.

Window seat: The window's wide sill is turned into a comfy seat by making a cushion to fit. Buy foam cut to size, then cover it with fabric, finishing the edges with cord trim for a professional look.

Furniture: The black bed frame stands out against the cool blues. Although not over-elaborate, its wrought-iron scrolls bring a hint of traditional style to the room, as does the old-fashioned radiator. Worn wooden furniture gives a laid-back look; the trunk near the bed is useful for storing bedlinen, while a cabinet has had its drawers painted blue to match the scheme.

Accessories: The juxtapositon of old and new continues with the accessories. An antique Ericsson telephone sits happily beside an ultra-modern clock radio. The picture above the bed is made up of a series of postcards on a background of plain white card.

The look: Zingy citrus yellow brings a wide-awake feel to this bedroom. While the colour scheme has an energetic, contemporary feel, the patchwork headboard, wooden blinds and wicker baskets on the wardrobe add hints of country charm to the room's corn-meadow freshness.

Colour: The enlivening citrus shade on the walls tones with the honey-coloured carpet to give an all-round glow. The fireplace, ceiling and wood-work are painted in a soft ivory, which reins in the sharp yellow while matching the colour of the large wardrobe. The cushions add accents of cool greens and warm pinks.

Headboard: An oversized headboard stands tall above the bed, its fabric cover made of plain and printed rectangles joined in patchwork fashion. If you make a loose cover, it will be easy to remove for washing: seam the patchwork panel along its top edge to another piece of fabric the same size, then hem all the raw edges. Stitch Velcro fastening down the side edges to hold it in place. Remember to allow extra for hems and turnings when cutting your panels.

Bedcoverings: Cosy textures bring a touch of warmth to the refreshing scheme. A woollen blanket and mohair throw join with knitted cushions to add comfort amid the cool cream and white bedlinen.

Furniture: Alcoves make useful storage areas, whether fitted with shelves or used to house freestanding furniture – the big wardrobe fits neatly into the space beside the fireplace. The MDF dressing table is painted to match the woodwork.

The look: In this room, bold squares featuring all the colours of the rainbow make a dramatic impact, putting the focus firmly on the bed. Pine furniture gives the scheme a warm, inviting feel.

Colour: If you want a look that packs a punch but are nervous about painting your walls in startling shades, do it the easy way by buying the brightest bedspread you can find. Then, if you change your mind about the colours, it's simpler to update your bedspread than repaint your walls! The understated natural colour of the wallpaper blends with the wooden furniture, providing a quiet backdrop that shows off the vibrantly coloured bedcover. The cushions and accessories add accents of green and dark blue.

Walls: The walls are covered with paper patterned to resemble a mottled, colourwashed effect. If you don't feel too confident with a paintbrush, special effects wallpapers like this are an alternative way of creating trendy paint finishes.

Curtains: The gathered curtains pick up on the colours of the bedspread but they are used in a less bold fashion – an all-over floral design – which coordinates with the border that runs around the top of the walls.

Furniture: If you like a coordinated look, invest in a complete set of matching furniture. These traditional-style pine pieces create a cosy country feel, which is enhanced by the wicker laundry trunk at the end of the bed.

The look: Bleached wood flooring, tongue-and-groove panelled walls and details such as the checked bedlinen and lacy tablecloth put this room in the country camp. However, the vivid wall colour and the simple white tiles used to cover the fireplace add a contemporary twist.

Colour: The turquoise used to paint the wooden wall panelling fills the room with cheerful colour. The bold stripes of the headboard and blind provide further colour interest, but the white bedlinen and tablecloth freshen the overall effect. Pale blue checks soften the dazzling contrast between the bedlinen and the walls.

Walls: Tongue-and-groove panelling is glued onto the walls all the way up to picture rail height. As well as giving a room a country feel, wood cladding is an effective way of concealing less-than-perfect plaster or textured paint that you can't face stripping.

Floor: The colour of the floorboards can affect the whole character of a room. These have a bleached effect that lightens the look, avoiding the oppressive feel that darker wood might create. Sanded boards can be given a similar look using a white woodwash. When dry, rub them down with beeswax and wire wool to give a gleaming finish.

Headboard: The home-made headboard has an MDF base which is padded with foam and covered with zingy striped fabric. The Roman blind at the window is made from the same material used vertically.

BEDROOM TIP
If you can't afford a new fire surround, tiling over an unused fireplace is a simple, low-cost solution. White tiles shine out against a coloured backdrop to give a clean, contemporary look

The look: The Van Gogh print on the far wall is the inspiration behind this room's smart monochrome scheme. However, this modern, masculine look also has a country complexion, thanks to romantic elements such as the pine bed and the softly draped sheer curtain.

Colour: The seamless backdrop of pure white walls and carpet combines with bold black accents and flashes of bright blue to fill the room with graphic contrasts. The silvery grey throw tones them down a little, but it's the blue-painted ceiling and the warm hues of the pine furniture that make the room feel cosy.

Ceiling: Few people think of turning their ceiling into an eye-catching feature, but a bedroom is one place where it's likely to be appreciated. This ceiling is decorated to create the impression of sleeping under the stars. Painted all over in deep blue, it is also stencilled with star motifs using metallic gold paint, and creates a dramatic impact among its all-white surroundings.

Furniture: A pine bed with heart-shaped cutout is just made for cute country style, but it also holds its own in this slicker contemporary setting. Along with the pine chest and battered wooden trunk, it gives the cool scheme a more relaxed feel. The director's chair is modern but casual, and stems of dried willow, although a contemporary accessory, have rustic overtones.

Window: Ethereal white sheers tied with bows to a black iron pole bring a romantic feel to the window, blending in with the white walls. A wooden Venetian blind provides greater privacy when required.

The look: Pine, the must-have wood of the 1980s, can be updated if you stick strictly to the less-is-more principle. Keep your room scheme plain and simple, and pine furniture will help to create a modern country feel without looking overly twee or cottagey.

Colour: The flaming deep orange on the walls makes a dramatic impact, and sets the scene for a scheme full of brilliant sunshine colours. Even the pillowcases are a vivid yellow, while a bedcover in fruity shades of tangerine, raspberry and lemon blends comfortably with the warm wood tones of the pine. The hot colours make for a cosy feel, but plain walls and simple checks keep the look modern.

Flooring: Wood flooring will add warmth to any room, and teams beautifully with hot colours such as reds and oranges, which enhance its natural glow. If your floorboards are in good condition, you can strip them by hiring sanding machines. If they are beyond repair, you can have new ones laid or, if you're skilled at DIY, buy some from a local timber merchant and lay them yourself.

Furniture: The pine furniture matches the floorboards to give a unified look. The drawer units provide plenty of storage space, but the single shelves are more for display, and a good way of adding interest to a large expanse of plainly painted wall. Look for shelves and brackets that are in character with your furniture, and use them to display decorative items such as pot plants, picture frames or candlesticks.

The look: Taking its inspiration straight from the African savannah, this scheme is based on the natural tones, textures and designs of traditional tribal art. A flowing bed canopy of gauzy net adds a touch of colonial romance.

Colour: For African style, colours should pick up on the earthy shades used in tribal designs, which originate from natural dyes. Include a mix of tones, from white and cream to terracotta and dark brown. In this room, mellow wall shades of mustard and cream provide a soothing backdrop for crisply laundered white bedlinen and dark wood flooring.

Bed: A mosquito net is great for making an instant bed canopy, and is particularly appropriate for an African look. Hang it from a hook in the ceiling and drape the fine netting around the head of your bed. Add a headboard made of natural materials: glue a sheet of split bamboo onto MDF, then screw chunky bamboo canes around the edges to finish.

Wardrobe: Panels of seagrass matting and bamboo finishing touches have adapted a junk-shop wardrobe to suit the scheme. The matting covers the spaces left by cutting panels of wood from the doors, and the bamboo is used to make handles and to trim the top of the unit.

Tribal art: Tribal prints and paintings are essential to this look. Jazz up an old ottoman by covering the lid with African-print canvas and the sides with seagrass matting. Paint your own tribal picture by copying traditional designs onto stretched canvas.

The look: It's back to basics with dramatic primary colours and solid metal furniture to create a retro 1950s feel. A pale backdrop and simple furniture keep the overall look contemporary, while country-style checks add a refreshing touch to relax the mood.

Colour: Pale creamy-yellow walls and a light wool and sisal carpet create a blank, space-enhancing canvas for the robust colours of the furniture and fabrics. A balanced mix of red, blue and green gives the scheme its impact, the checks of the curtains and blanket adding lively pattern to break up the bold blocks of colour.

Furniture: All the furniture is made of metal, and the lines are clean and contemporary, leaving it to the colours to give the room its retro feel. The bright red cabinet made of lacquered steel might seem an unusual choice for a bedroom, but it is ideal for this scheme and is just the right height to provide useful display space as well as storage capacity.

Window: The gathered curtains add a softer touch to offset the hard metals, their country-style green checks echoing the larger squares of the cosy woollen blanket on the bed. Adding a deep valance across the top helps to give the drapes more impact by framing the wide window. The nickel curtain pole matches the metal furniture and tones with the cool greens.

Accessories: Continue the metallic theme with shiny galvanized jugs and containers, and look for accessories in the key colours of your scheme. A 1950s-style radio is guaranteed to enhance the retro look.

Colour: The curtain fabric is the inspiration behind this room's blend of bright blue, lilac and lime green, colours that create a refreshing but relaxing atmosphere. The deeper-toned cobalt carpet adds warmth and comfort at floor level, while the top of the walls and the ceiling have been kept white to give the illusion of height.

Pattern: Instead of going for a totally coordinated look with fabrics from the same range as the curtains, the owners have chosen a mix of designs in similar colours for a more individual look. The blue of the curtains is repeated in the duvet cover, while the embroidered lime-green bedspread incorporates all the colours of the room in its large floral design.

Furniture: Wood and wicker furniture has a natural home-spun feel that adds to the relaxed air. The sturdy wooden wardrobe provides ample storage and, with its panelled doors and carved detailing,

has more character than many fitted modern units. Striped cardboard boxes provide additional storage on top.

Fireplace: Once hidden beneath layers of plywood, the original 1920s fireplace has been unmasked and restored using gunmetal polish.

Accessories: Put soul into your scheme with a few well-chosen accessories that each add their own individual touch. The painting on the mantelpiece gives the room an arty feel, the pink heart-shaped cushion on an old school chair adds a vampish note, and the toy snake, curling around the top of the wardrobe, introduces a hint of childish fun.

BEDROOM TIP
If your walls have attractive original details, such as picture rails or coving, you may prefer freestanding furniture because it will not conceal them as thoroughly as would a wall-to-wall fitted storage system

The look: It's the details that count in this room, where ribbon edgings and bows turn white bedlinen from plain to pretty to create a delightfully feminine look.

Colour: Choose all-white furniture and bedlinen, and the colour palette is your oyster when it comes to choosing ribbon trim. This room mixes candy colours such as pink and lilac with soft aquas and greens in ginghams and girly florals, but you'll find a vast range of colours and styles in haberdashery stores. For the walls, pick out a colour from the ribbons – a mid-tone will provide a good contrast for white furnishings.

Bedlinen: White bedlinen is cheap to buy and easy to embellish. Give pillowcases a lift with borders of ribbon and braid. Cut it a bit longer than you need, then pin in place, turning under the ends to neaten, and sew close to both edges. Sew ribbons to the open edges of the pillowcase and tie in bows. Pretty up a plain duvet cover with bows: cut 40cm lengths of ribbon, knot each in the centre and tie in a bow. Pin to the cover and sew the knots in place.

Accessories: Use similar ribbon trim to decorate accessories. Cover a plain lampshade with stripes of narrow ribbon in two contrasting colours – mark evenly spaced lines on the shade, then stick on the ribbon using double-sided tape. Cut floral braid to fit around the rims and fix with a glue gun, overlapping the ends. Decorate towels in the same way as the pillowcases, by sewing on ribbon and braid.

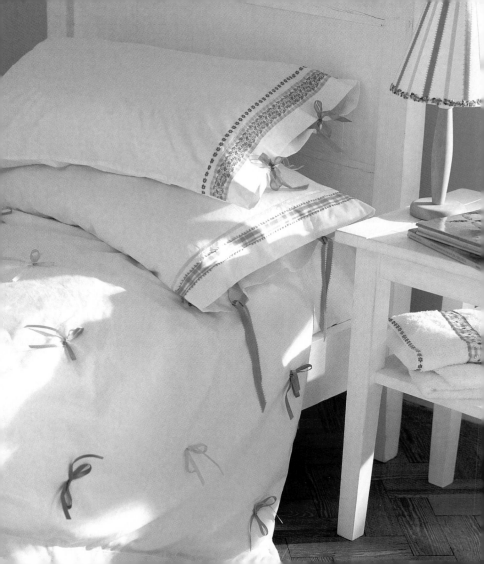

The look: Packed with spriggy floral prints in pretty pastel colours, this room has a retro 1950s look with a very feminine feel. The shapely antique bed and old-fashioned telephone add to the nostalgic appeal of the scheme.

Colour: Girly pastel shades of fresh yellow and pink form the basis of the look, while a brighter turquoise bedcover and liberal splashes of bold red strengthen the overall effect. Keeping the background plain helps to offset the fussiness of the floral furnishings. The pale yellow of the walls tones with the neutral-coloured carpeting and cream-painted woodwork to give a seamless look.

Fabrics: Crisp 1950s-style cottons peppered with tiny flowers and buds define the retro theme. Quilted bedspreads and a genuine 1950s eiderdown enhance the vintage charm of the florals. Layering the bed with covers and cushions in a mix of plains and different patterns gives an individual look.

Bed: The antique wooden bed, with its beautiful curves and carved floral detailing, has been re-upholstered in a rose fabric to match the other 1950s-style prints in the room.

Storage: With shelves and a rail fitted for clothes, a wide alcove provides all the storage facilities of a wardrobe. Wicker baskets and flower-patterned boxes house smaller items. A curtain trimmed with gingham and bright pink ribbon screens the contents of the alcove from view, while adding another floral print to the mix.

Colour: Painting the walls and ceiling entirely in cream not only increases the illusion of space and light in a room but also provides a blank canvas that allows you to be more creative with colour when it comes to furnishings and accessories. Three bold and contrasting contemporary shades highlight key features of this room: sharp lime green and turquoise on the bed and a cheerful orange for the curtains and wall-mounted display box.

Furniture: If you're starting from scratch, you may want to choose a set of furniture that conforms to one style, but many of us already have a mixture of different pieces collected over the years. An eclectic selection of furniture can work well against a plain contemporary backdrop. This room includes an interesting mix of styles, from the sturdy old wooden chest and elegant full-length mirror to the modern iron bed, silver wicker chair and futuristic flying saucer light shade.

Display boxes: Small box-like shelves, easy to make from MDF, provide a frame effect that's ideal for showing off treasured accessories. With their neat, modern style, the boxes are also a feature in themselves, especially when painted in an eye-catching colour, and add interest to large expanses of plain wall. Let the items you want to display dictate the size and shape of the boxes, so that each accessory has its own purpose-made showcase.

Curtains: Orange sheers frame the window with warm sunny colour, at the same time as letting plenty of light filter through their fine fabric. The full, flowing drapes add a touch of romance and welcome softness to the scheme.

BEDROOM TIP
Give an old wicker chair a new lease of life with spray paint. Silver will bring it bang up to date with a look of high-tech glamour. Work in a well-ventilated room and cover surrounding surfaces with plenty of newspaper

The look: The reproduction bed, original fireplace and striking Regency-style wall stripes give this room a look of classical French elegance. However, it is far from formal, with the refreshingly simple blue and white colour scheme, rustic wooden floorboards and light window dressing working together to relax the mood.

Colour: A crisp combination of blue and white will bring a fresh feel to any room. The natural wood tones of the polished pine floorboards and furniture help to take off the chill, while deep blue lamps and glassware add a more intense dose of colour.

Wall stripes: The marquee-style stripes were inspired by those on the bed. Applying the blue as a colourwash gives the stripes a softer, less regimental effect than painting on solid colour. Mask off each stripe, using a plumbline to get the lines vertical, then paint on diluted emulsion using rough, random brushstrokes designed to give uneven coverage.

Furniture: A bed is usually the focal point of a bedroom, so it can be well worth investing in something distinctive. This is a reproduction of a French Louis XVI design. Other furniture has been kept simple and practical, in natural pine or white-painted wood. The two wardrobes fit neatly into alcoves beside the chimney breast.

Window: With such lively stripes on the walls, it's best to opt for a simple window treatment. The delicate white curtains are complemented by a slender iron curtain pole with curly finials.

The look: Bristling with scrolls and swirls, this scheme was inspired by the Art Nouveau period. A purple and black colour scheme provides a flamboyant backdrop for the riot of patterns.

Colour: White flooring helps to tone down the powerful effect of the purple walls, with their lively border of swirls stencilled in mauve. Touches of black have the effect of smartening up a scheme. Used for the woodwork, it adds definition to details such as the picture rail, and also outlines the walls, sharpening the strong contrast with the clean white floor.

Furniture: Apart from the white iron bed, all the furniture is embellished with swirls. The black-painted chest of drawers has a big scroll fretwork handle cut from MDF and sprayed with copper metallic paint. It is fixed in place with pieces of dowelling and sawn through so that the drawers can open. The tall lampstands were specially made for the room, again from MDF.

Windows: You don't need wide windows to indulge in dramatic dressings. Black-painted pelmets specially cut from MDF frame these tall, narrow windows, while purple curtains in a luxurious plushy fabric are swept back in grand fashion.

Accessories: Glamorous details abound: a pair of period-style lamps with silk shades, a stunning mirror frame and plenty of candles. Piles of purple velvet cushions add sumptuous comfort to the bed, while the white cushions are printed with peacock feathers, a favourite Art Nouveau motif.

The look: With the stunning blood-red sky effect on the walls, this bedroom pays homage to the opening scene of the film *Bram Stoker's Dracula*, where the rising sun turns into a ball of fire. The gold-painted fireplace and the ornate period-style furniture enhance the Gothic feeling. Accessories are few and the bedlinen is plain so as not to distract attention from the walls.

Colour: As intended, the brilliant fiery colours used on the walls and ceiling dominate the room to create a gloriously theatrical effect. This is heightened by contrast with the clean white bedlinen, and intensified by the vivid magenta carpet, a continuation of the pinkish tones that blend with the reds at the base of the walls.

Walls: To give the effect of a streaked dawn sky, the walls have been spray-painted in fuzzy, horizontal bands of intense red, orange and yellow, which have been cleverly blended and shaped to look like clouds.

Fireplace: The plaster surround of the original fireplace is decorated with metallic gold paint, which matches the skirting boards and complements the glowing tones of the walls. An unexpected finish for a period fireplace, the glitzy gold enhances the fantasy feel of the room.

Furniture: The Edwardian-style bedstead is made of steel with a black finish, and has gleaming brass knobs with an antiqued look that echoes the gold-painted woodwork. The old-fashioned mirror frame on the mantelpiece and the traditional style and heavy dark wood of the ornately carved chair in the corner sit well with the Dracula theme.

The look: This room combines the upholstered luxury and rich colours of a classical setting with the clean lines of contemporary style. The result is a look that gives uncluttered modernity a cosier face.

Colour: The traditional shade of green used on the walls creates a serene backdrop for the blocks of rich, warm colour – mustard and red – used for the bedcover and headboard. Painting one wall in cream lightens the overall look.

Bed: The bed is an ordinary divan, its base concealed by a red valance. If you're short of storage space, look for a divan fitted with drawers in the base where you can stash bedlinen or out-of-season clothes to keep the room tidy. Covering the whole of the bed, including the pillows, gives a neat look. Sew your own bedspread and you can choose any colours you like – this one is made from panels of curtain lining fabric. Decorative cushions in more

sumptuous red and gold fabrics add a touch of glamour.

Headboard: The big squashy headboard is made from foam pillows that sit, without sagging, inside pillowcases. They hang from a simple dowelling rod that slots into cup hooks fixed to the wall.

Shelves: Narrow shelves are fixed above the bed and on the near wall. Painted to match the walls, the shelves themselves remain unobtrusive, but they provide display space where decorative accessories can add a personal touch to the plain scheme.

BEDROOM TIP
If you're looking for luxurious fabrics to make cushion covers, remember to search the remnants bins in fabric stores. You can often pick up offcuts of silks and velvets at a fraction of the full price

Colour: Rich berry reds contrast with cool cream for a look that's as cosy as it is modern. Using deep red on both the walls and the sloping ceiling maximizes the feeling of warmth. To add subtle pattern, the wall behind the bed is stencilled with a circular design, applied using gloss varnish. White-painted floorboards lift the overall look, and fluffy flokati rugs give them a more comfortable feel.

Bed: The clever MDF structure built around the divan bed turns it into an imposing focal point, and provides handy shelf space at the head and foot. The fabric-covered flap at the head also lifts up to reveal a mirror, plus storage space inside for cosmetics. A strip of the same fabric sewn to the bedcover continues the panel of pattern to break up the expanse of strong red.

Window: Wooden shutters provide a neat dressing for the tiny window. Each one is prettied up with a painted-on panel of real rose petals. Mix the petals into a solution of one part water to three parts PVA adhesive, then brush it onto the shutter. When the glue is dry, seal your decoration with a coat of diluted PVA.

Bedside lamps: The tall lamps make an eye-catching feature. To make one, cut a timber post into a column shape, then glue and nail it to a larger square of MDF. Paint the wood with emulsion, then varnish. Wire a flex to a bottletop adaptor, and fix the adaptor to the top of the post. Fix a shade and bulb to the adaptor.

BEDROOM TIP
Tall bedside lamps are best for reading in bed as they cast a pool of light down onto the book. Always fit lamps on both sides of a double bed so that each partner can control their own lighting level without disturbing the other

Colour: Mediterranean colours bring a warm glow to this loft bedroom. The burnt orange emulsion on the walls is broken up with cream-coloured stripes, which match the paintwork on the screen and bedhead, but it's the vibrant colours that dominate. Many of us fight shy of combining boldly clashing hues, but when used as blocks of colour in a simple modern scheme they can create a look full of impact.

Wall stripes: If you want light-coloured stripes on a darker wall, paint the stripes first. Apply the lighter paint roughly, then stick wide masking tape on top of the stripes and paint over this with the darker emulsion.

Screen: A huge curved screen divides the room into two distinct areas, for sleeping and dressing. Curving around one corner of the bed, it is made from flexible plywood nailed to a timber frame and painted in cream-coloured emulsion.

Bed: The bed has been updated with modern posts. Saw off your old bedposts and make new ones by threading painted timber cubes onto lengths of dowelling drilled into the bed. The gold bedspread is painted with square motifs, applied using scarlet fabric paint.

Mirror: The circular mirror is framed with gold mosaic tiles. Glue a round mirror to a larger circle of MDF, then stick on the mosaics using tile adhesive. When this is dry, apply grey grout, filling all the gaps between the tiles. The shelf below the mirror, a slab of slate resting on two plaster corbels, is ideal for holding toiletries or displaying decorative accessories.

The look: A bedroom is a very personal space, which should be decorated to please only its owners. It's the one room where fantasies can be indulged, even if that means going wild with brilliant tiger stripes on the walls and leopard spots on the ceiling. With its eye-popping colour and jumble of diverse accessories, this highly individualistic look is full of fun.

Colour: Crammed with colour and pattern, this is a room that can't fail to stimulate the senses. Startling wall stripes in flame colours team with the orange tones of the wooden floorboards to create a glowing atmosphere. The stripes are deliberately uneven, their waviness giving a looser, more creative feel than straight edges. Pattern power continues on the ceiling with its wacky covering of leopard spots, echoed by the muslin curtains, and on the bed with its colourful checked quilt and blue cover with childish Noah's Ark print.

Furniture: As with colour, almost anything goes when it comes to furniture, although minimalist lines would probably not appeal to the owner of this room! Curly wrought iron and wicker suit the decorative theme. A sofa upholstered with yet another print, and piled with cushions in many colours, creates a comfortable corner.

Accessories: A varied collection of unusual treasures, from a pair of leopard-print boots to a classical statue, add to the quirky feel of the room. The elaborate mirror frame is a DIY creation made from MDF and painted with cherubs and shells.

The look: The palest blush of pink creates a light and pretty contemporary bedroom. Saris with glitzy gold borders have been put to imaginative use as soft furnishings, adding a hint of laid-back glamour.

Colour: Pale pink paint on both the walls and floorboards gives a spacious feel, making the large room feel especially bright and airy. A lively mint green highlights the window frames, drawing attention to the attractive bay while offsetting the sugary quality of the pink. The vibrancy of the exotic pink bedlinen defines the bed as the focal point of the room.

Soft furnishings: Saris make excellent value-for-money furnishings – each one includes several metres of fabric and they often feature luxurious trimmings or embroidery. Look for them in fabric stores or markets in the Indian quarters of big cities. The duvet cover and matching pillowcases are made from a bright pink, gold-trimmed sari, and the addition of a cream sari throw softens the impact of this hot colour. More cream saris have been made into curtains; lining them with white cotton ensures adquate privacy at the ground-floor window.

Furniture: A mixture of wooden furniture gives a natural, easy-going look. The alcove shelves are painted pink to make them fade into the background.

Fireplace: If your budget won't stretch to a new fire surround, conceal an ugly fireplace by making a simple but smart MDF version. Paint it to blend in with the walls for a clean, modern look.

BEDROOM TIP
Use lighting to add a decorative touch as well as alter the mood of a room. Rescue those fairy lights from the Christmas decorations box and string them along a plain mantelpiece to add magical sparkle all year round

The look: Colour fun gives this room its bright, modern look. Clear contemporary shades of lilac and lime create a striking contrast on neighbouring walls, but it's the dolly-mixture colours on the furniture that really pack a punch. They give the scheme an almost childish feel, which is enhanced by the *Sesame Street* puppets scattered around the room.

Furniture: Basic wooden furniture with clean lines suits a modern scheme, and is cheap to buy. Add character by decorating it – these pieces have been transformed with colour. Even the bed is painted a bold fuchsia pink, while the chest of drawers alternates this shade with deep purple for true colour power.

Bedlinen: Simple bedcoverings reinforce the minimalist feel of the room. The soft greens and thin purple stripe of the duvet cover and pillowcases complement all the other colours in the room without overpowering the scheme. The checks add an element of cheery pattern.

Carpet: With so many bright colours, a neutral carpet makes a calming base. The floor represents a large area of any room, so take care when choosing carpeting – a strong shade may dominate your scheme or fight with other colours in the room. A carpet is often an investment buy, so a neutral tone will allow for greater flexibility if you decide to change your colour scheme.

Pictures: A sheet of giftwrap displayed in an aluminium frame creates an inexpensive picture. Fixed to board using spray adhesive, its colourful spotted design makes a graphic statement. The picture above the bed is an old movie poster.

Cost: This bedroom cost just £500 to transform – with a few clever DIY ideas thrown in. The carpet and furniture are cheap high-street buys, plain bedlinen has been tarted up with remnants of luxury fabric and the walls are painted to give the look of wallpaper.

Walls: If you like wallpaper but can't afford it, try using paints to create special effects. The textured look on the wall behind the bed has been achieved using a jeans-effect paint. The oval motifs on the left wall are stamped on – check out your local DIY or craft store for a wide range of stamp designs.

Furniture: Think solid for your bed frame and you'll get quality and value rolled into one. The big headboard, which doubles as a shelf, is made from painted MDF. The chest of drawers and bedside table are cheap melamine pieces which have been updated by painting, then gluing strips of beading and panels of linen fabric onto the doors and drawers. The handles are wrapped with string to continue the natural look.

Bedlinen: Look for exotic silky fabric in markets and use it to trim a plain white duvet cover or bedspread and to make cushion covers that add an aura of luxury to your bed.

Window dressings: Two light bargain window treatments can look more effective than one heavier, higher-priced blind or curtain. Here a paper blind is layered with fine curtains in a cheap and cheerful fabric. When used together, they do an adequate job of shutting out light at dawn.

BEDROOM TIP
To paint melamine furniture, you must first apply a suitable primer, otherwise your topcoat won't stick to the smooth surface. Look for melamine primer at DIY stores. Some multi-surface primers may also work on melamine, but check the details on the can before buying

The look: This scheme combines bold blocks of colour for a fun, paintbox-bright effect. Using colour is one of the most affordable ways to give a room character, so think how you can use it creatively. In this room, the walls remain white while each of the other features contributes a different shade to the mix.

Colour: The bedspread forms the inspiration for the scheme – the shades used for the furniture and furnishings are all picked out from its rainbow checks. A bright blue covers the bed frame, while the darker background of the artwork contrasts with the golden yellow curtains. Painting a door can turn it into an eye-catching feature. This one has been transformed with brilliant pink, plus a contrasting green handle. The natural tones of the wicker trunk and wooden flooring rein in the colour burst to add a homely feel.

Furniture: Painting furniture can give it a unique look – an ordinary pine bed takes on a more upbeat character when decorated in vivid blue, while the simple bedside chest also gets a colour lift with drawers in emerald green. Sand down wooden furniture to give a key for the paint before applying the colour of your choice. Gloss, satinwood and eggshell give a hard-wearing finish on wood. Use emulsion for a matt appearance and top with a durable varnish.

Artwork: Used as a colour tool, a painted canvas is great for brightening up a dull corner. Create your own using simple shapes and just a few colours that suit your scheme. Ready-stretched canvases are available from art shops.

Colour: Making a bold colour statement, this room's far wall is painted in two vibrantly contrasting hues, which are echoed by the two-toned bedspread. The remaining walls and ceiling have been left white, to lend impact to the colour. The glowing wood tones of the polished floorboards blend with the warm orange and yellows.

Wall: If you want to save money on paint but love colour, decorate just one wall to form an attention-grabbing focal point. The centre of this wall was painted with vivid yellow, then a border of eye-popping pink was roughly applied around it. Hanging a picture in the centre emphasizes the frame effect.

Bedspread: A two-tone bedspread has been made by dyeing half a plain one. Use cold water or hand dyes, which are available from craft and haberdashery stores and work best on natural fabrics such as cotton or linen. Check that your fabric is suitable for dyeing, then weigh it to find out how many packs of dye you need. Mix the dye and fixative following the manufacturer's instructions, then dip in half the bedspread and leave for the required time. Hang up to drip dry.

Storage area: The storage area is screened by old chenille drapes in a traditional dark red, a shift of style from the modern treatment of the adjoining wall.

Furniture: The furniture is an eclectic mix of old and new. The red bed is in tune with the zappy colour effects, while the old chest of drawers and battered suitcase under the bed suggest a more lived-in feel.

BEDROOM TIP
If you're short of wall space but want to fit in a chest of drawers, remember that you can place a low one against the end of the bed

The look: If you can live with very little furniture, one way of keeping your decorating within budget is to opt for a minimalist look. This clutter-free loft room holds just a bed and a window seat, both DIY creations. The stark decor, with its bold splashes of colour, adds to the hard-edged modern feel.

Colour: Walls painted mainly in pure white suit the clean, minimalist theme and maximize the feeling of light and space in the loft room. Colour is used to highlight key features such as the window alcove, which is painted in lime green and home to a bright blue window seat. To add an industrial touch, the skirting boards and radiator are decorated with metallic aluminium-coloured paint.

Flooring: The only major expense in this room was the silvery rubber floor tiles. To provide a solid base, hardboard was nailed to the bare floorboards. Applying adhesive to both the hardboard and the tiles ensures a strong bond.

Bed: To save splashing out on a new bed, a DIY base has been made for an existing mattress using MDF and timber. The MDF sides, sealed with PVA adhesive, have slate tiles glued on top using tile adhesive. Castors screwed to each corner make it easy to move the bed around the room. A hard-wearing throw in bargain-buy indigo denim is the perfect industrial-style cover.

Window seat: The seat beneath the window, which doubles as a side table, is made from MDF painted in blue and lime-green emulsion, then varnished. Like the bed, it is fitted with castors for full mobility.

BEDROOM TIP

Fitting wheels to furniture gives your room scheme greater flexibility by taking the strain out of changing the layout. Look for lockable castors so that your furniture stays put when you need it to

The look: Refreshing greens and a mix of wood tones bring the shades of nature into this room, but the plain colour scheme and smart checks keep the country influence under control, making the overall effect one of relaxed modern simplicity and calm.

Colour: Lime green gives the walls a fresh, contemporary feel. As a cool colour, it enhances the feeling of space, but is best used in a room that gets sufficient natural daylight. There is an old saying that blue and green should never be seen together but they actually make a comfortably balanced combination. The deep blues of the bedspread and futon take away the acid quality of the lime green, while the checked cushion and throw add darker and lighter shades of green to bring all-important tonal variation into the scheme.

Futon: Ideal for providing extra sleeping space when family or friends come to stay, a futon is a cheaper option than most sofa beds. It has a casual, contemporary appearance, hard-wearing, washable cotton upholstery and a wooden frame that goes well with the pine bed in this room.

Furniture: The pine bed and blond wood of the shelving echo the varied tones of the floorboards to add a relaxed, natural feel to the room. Low-cost pine furniture is widely available from large DIY stores and furniture chains.

Blind: If you want to continue the look of natural wood as far as the window, a narrow-slatted pinoleum blind is more affordable than wooden Venetians or shutters. It lets light filter through even when lowered for privacy.

BEDROOM TIP
Don't crowd out a small spare room with a double bed, especially if you have to place one of its sides against a wall. A single bed and futon combination frees up floor space and also provides more flexibility for sleeping arrangements

Colour: A medley of contemporary aquas, blues and lilacs makes a cool, harmonious combination. Using them as blocks of colour on both the walls and furniture adds interest to the overall look. The walls are painted in a pale shade of aqua, and mid-tones of aqua and lilac have been used on the fitted wardobe doors. The much stronger blue of the freestanding cupboard completes the variation of tones from light to dark.

Furniture: Large wardrobe doors can look boring and imposing, but painting them in different colours helps them to earn their place in the scheme. Complete the revamp by fitting new handles that reflect the style of your room. Don't feel you have to paint every bit of furniture though – elements of natural wood can add a comforting natural touch amid a mix of colours.

Bedlinen: Plain white bedlinen freshens the look and is also affordable. To jazz it up and create a colour link with the rest of the room, trim it with gingham ribbon in dark blue and white. Cheap but luxurious sari silks have been made into cushions that echo the colours of the walls and furniture.

Picture: Decorative details are important in any room, but there's no need to pay gallery prices for works of art. DIY paintings may not be up to Picasso standards, but when viewed as a feature of a room scheme they can add colour and character. The picture above the bed was made by sticking a sheet of geometric-design giftwrap to MDF using spray adhesive.

The look: This scheme might appear to be oozing elegance but is actually the result of a speedy makeover carried out on a strict budget. Old furniture has been revamped, cool colours chosen to create a feeling of space and calm, and glamorous classic-style details added as finishing touches.

Colour: The combination of muted blue walls with clean white bedlinen and furniture creates a scheme that's both restful and refreshing. Natural sisal flooring adds a third colour to the mix, while the black fire surround and picture frames smarten up the scheme by punctuating it with dashes of a darker tone.

Furniture: The old chest of drawers and the dressing table have been revived with a coat of primer and a lick of white paint in a satin finish. Details make all the difference – the ornate edges of the dressing table have been glammed up with gold paint and the drawers fitted with pretty resin handles. The chest also has new blue glass drawer knobs.

Window: To ensure privacy, a double blind effect was created. Behind the fabric panel is a simple white woven roller blind. The sheer muslin panel is more decorative than functional; its stripes bring together both main colours of the scheme, and its floor-skimming floatiness adds a touch of romance.

Accessories: Clear glass vases and accessories, such as the finials of the curtain pole and the droplets of the chandelier, strike an elegant note.

STOCKISTS:

ONE-STOP SHOPS

DEBENHAMS
Furniture, bedlinen, window
dressings and lighting.
Tel: 020 7408 4444
www.debenhams.com

FREEMANS
Furniture, bedlinen, window
dressings and lighting.
Tel: 0800 900200
www.freemans.com

HABITAT
Contemporary furniture,
bedlinen, and lighting.
Tel: 0845 601 0740
www.habitat.net

HEAL'S
Contemporary furniture,
bedlinen, fabrics and lighting.
Tel: 020 7636 1666
www.heals.co.uk

IKEA
Affordable flatpack furniture;
furnishings, fabrics and lighting.
Tel: 020 8208 5600
www.ikea.co.uk

JOHN LEWIS
Wide range of furniture, fabrics,
bedlinen, window dressings and
lighting. Carpet fitting service.
Tel: 020 7629 7711
www.johnlewis.co.uk

LAURA ASHLEY
Classic and country-style
furniture, fabrics, window
dressings, lighting and paints.
Tel: 0870 562 2116 for stockists,
0800 868100 for mail order
www.lauraashley.com

MARKS & SPENCER
Classic and modern furniture,
curtains, bedlinen and lighting.
Tel: 020 7935 4422 for stockists,
0845 603 1603 for mail order
www.marks-and-spencer.com

NEXT HOME
Furniture, bedlinen, wallpaper,
paints, curtains and lighting.
Tel: 0870 243 5435 for stockists,
0845 600 7000 for mail order
www.next.co.uk

AND SO TO BED
Wood, brass and iron beds in traditional designs.
Tel: 020 7731 3593
www.andsotobed.co.uk

ART IN IRON
Contemporary iron beds and matching bedside tables.
Tel: 020 7924 2332
www.zzz4u.com

BEAVER & TAPLEY
Freestanding modular storage units in real wood finishes.
Tel: 0845 606 0340
www.beaverandtapley.co.uk

BED BAZAAR
Antique metal bedsteads from all periods restored and sold.
Tel: 01728 724944

THE CONRAN SHOP
Contemporary designer furniture.
Tel: 020 7589 7401
www.conran.co.uk

COURTS
Divans, bedsteads and futons.
Tel: 020 8640 3322
www.courts.co.uk

CROWN IMPERIAL
Fully fitted storage furniture made to measure.
Tel: 01227 742424
www.crown-imperial.co.uk

THE DORMY HOUSE
Blanket boxes and tables sold ready to paint; headboards upholstered to order.
Tel: 01264 365789
www.thedormyhouse.com

DUCAL
Solid wood furniture in traditional designs, including four posters.
Tel: 01264 333666
www.ducal-furniture.co.uk

FUTON COMPANY
Futon sofa beds, simple screens and canvas-covered wardrobes.
Tel: 0845 609 4455

GRAND ILLUSIONS
French country-style furniture, painted, distressed or waxed.
Tel: 020 8607 9446
www.maison.com

HAMMONDS FURNITURE
Fully fitted storage systems made to measure.
Tel: 01455 251451

THE HOLDING COMPANY
Contemporary storage furniture and accessories.
Tel: 020 7610 9160
www.theholdingcompany.co.uk

IN N OUT TRADING
Oriental chests, screens and tables in dark wood and iron.
Tel: 020 8452 0300
www.innout.co.uk

THE IRON BED COMPANY
Iron beds in classic and contemporary styles.
Tel: 01243 578888
www.ironbed.co.uk

JAY-BE
Beds, sofa beds, folding beds.
Tel: 01924 517820 for stockists, 01924 517822 for brochure.
www.jaybe.co.uk

LLOYD LOOM OF SPALDING
Woven fibre furniture, including the classic Lloyd Loom chairs.
Tel: 01775 712111
www.lloydloom.com

MAGNET
Fitted and freestanding furniture. Over 500 branches nationwide – contact local branch for details.
www.magnet.co.uk

MARKS & SPENCER
Classic and modern furniture.
Tel: 020 7935 4422 for stockists, 0845 603 1603 for mail order
www.marks-and-spencer.com

MFI
Affordable furniture suites in solid pine or wood finishes.
Tel: 0870 241 0154
www.mfi.co.uk

NORDIC STYLE
Painted wooden furniture in classic Swedish designs.
Tel: 020 7351 1755

THE PIER
Ethnic-style furniture ranges in dark wood, bamboo and rattan.
Tel: 020 7814 5020 for stockists, 020 7814 5004 for mail order
www.pier.co.uk

RELYON
Traditional bedsteads in forged iron, cast metal and brass.
Tel: 01823 667501
www.relyon.co.uk

SCUMBLE GOOSIE
Ready-to-paint furniture in classic designs.
Tel: 01453 731315
www.scumblegoosie.com

SHARPS BEDROOMS
Fully fitted storage systems made to measure.
Tel: 0800 917 8178

SLEEPEEZEE
Divan beds, including the backcare collection.
Tel: 020 8540 9171

SLUMBERLAND
Divan beds, headboards, mattresses and sofa beds.
Tel: 0161 628 2898
www.slumberland.co.uk

SOFAS AND SOFA-BEDS
Sofas and sofa beds upholstered to order.
Tel: 020 7637 1932
www.sofaweb.co.uk

STUART BUGLASS IRONWORKS
Classic and modern iron beds, curtain poles and light fittings.
Tel: 01604 890366
www.stuartbuglass.co.uk

WICKES
Affordable fitted furniture supplied ready for DIY assembly.
Tel: 0870 608 9001
www.wickes.co.uk

PAINTS

AURO ORGANIC PAINTS
Paints and woodstains made from natural products.
Tel: 01799 543077
www.auroorganic.co.uk

B&Q
Contemporary colours, plus Benetton special effects paints.
Tel: 020 7576 6502
www.diy.com

CROWN PAINTS
Vast choice, including the mix-to-order Expressions collection.
Tel: 01254 704951
www.crownpaint.co.uk

DULUX
Vast choice of shades in many ranges, including the extensive Colour Mixing System.
Tel: 01753 550555
www.dulux.co.uk

FARROW & BALL
Heritage paint shades.
Tel: 01202 876141
www.farrow-ball.co.uk

FIRED EARTH
Neutral and traditional colours.
Tel: 01295 814300
www.firedearth.com

HOMEBASE
Wide choice, including ranges
by Jane Churchill and Laura
Ashley.
Tel: 0870 900 8098
www.homebase.co.uk

INTERNATIONAL PAINT
Paints and primers for
melamine, radiators and floors;
also tile and speciality paints.
Tel: 01962 711177
www.international-paints.co.uk

SANDERSON
More than 1,000 mix-to-order
colours in the Spectrum range.
Tel: 01895 830000
www.sanderson-uk.com

ZEST
Vibrant Mediterranean colours.
Tel: 020 7351 7674
www.zestessentials.com

DECORATIVE EFFECTS

CREATIVE BEADCRAFT
Wide range of beads.
Tel: 01494 715606
www.creativebeadcraft.co.uk

DYLON
Fabric dyes in many colours.
Tel: 020 8663 4296
www.dylon.co.uk

THE ENGLISH STAMP COMPANY
Wall stamps and stamping tools.
Tel: 01929 439117
www.englishstamp.com

HAMMERITE
Metallic paints and enamels.
Tel: 01661 830000
www.hammerite.com

HOMECRAFTS DIRECT
Craft products by mail order.
Tel: 0116 269 7733
www.homecrafts.co.uk

HUMBROL
Makers of Glass Etch spray
(for a frosted effect on glass).
Tel: 01482 701191

LIBERON
Waxes and other wood finishes.
Tel: 01797 367555

THE PAINTED FINISH
Paint effects products and tools.
Tel: 01926 842376
www.craftychick.com

PÉBÉO
Fabric and porcelain paints.
Tel: 02380 701144
www.pebeo.com

STENCIL LIBRARY
Stencils and stencilling tools.
Tel: 01661 844844
www.stencil-library.com

SPECIALIST CRAFTS
Wide range of craft products.
Tel: 0116 269 7711 for stockists,
0116 269 7733 for mail order
www.speccrafts.co.uk

VV ROULEAUX
Ribbons, braids and trimmings.
Tel: 020 7434 3899
www.vvrouleaux.com

ANDREW MARTIN
Printed fabrics and wallpapers,
velvets, suedes and leather.
Tel: 020 7225 5100 for stockists.

ANNA FRENCH
Floral and paint-effect
wallpapers; printed cotton
fabrics, lace and sheers.
Tel: 020 7349 1099

CATH KIDSTON
Retro 1950s-style floral cottons.
Tel: 020 7221 4000 for stockists,
020 7229 8000 for mail order
www.cathkidston.co.uk

COLEFAX & FOWLER
Beautiful florals on linen and
chintz, and an extensive range of
weaves and wallpapers.
Tel: 020 8877 6400

COLOROLL
Contemporary wallcoverings
and coordinating bedlinen.
Tel: 0800 056 4878
www.coloroll.co.uk

**CROWN WALLCOVERINGS &
HOME FURNISHINGS**
Wide range of wallcoverings.
Tel: 0800 458 1554
www.ihdg.co.uk

FABRICS AND WALLPAPERS

DESIGNERS GUILD
Colourful contemporary
fabrics, wallpapers, paints
and bedlinen.
Tel: 020 7351 5775
www.designersguild.com

GRAHAM & BROWN
Contemporary wallcoverings,
including textures and
metallics.
Tel: 0800 3288452
www.grahambrown.com

IAN MANKIN
Natural fabrics in plains,
stripes and checks, including
plenty of classic tickings and
ginghams.
Tel: 020 7722 0997

JANE CHURCHILL FABRICS
Wallpapers, cottons and linens
with floral and geometric
designs in light, contemporary
colours.
Tel: 020 8877 6400

JOHN LEWIS
Fabrics and wallpapers from
many different suppliers.
Tel: 020 7629 7711
www.johnlewis.com

KA INTERNATIONAL
Pure cottons in vibrant colours.
Tel: 020 7584 7352
www.ka-international.com

KNICKERBEAN
Discount stores with designer
fabrics at bargain prices.
Tel: 01842 751327

LAURA ASHLEY
Classic and country-style
fabrics and papers, especially
florals.
Tel: 0870 562 2116 for stockists,
0800 868100 for mail order
www.lauraashley.com

MALABAR
Hand-woven silks and cotton
fabrics imported from India.
Tel: 020 7501 4200
www.malabar.co.uk

THE MODERN SAREE CENTRE
Sarees and Indian silks.
Tel: 020 7247 4040

THE NATURAL FABRIC COMPANY
Wide range of natural fabrics,
from hessian and calico to
chambray and sheers.
Tel: 01488 684002

OSBORNE & LITTLE
Classic and contemporary
prints, weaves and wallpapers.
Tel: 020 7352 1456
www.osborneandlittle.com

SANDERSON
Coordinated fabric, wallcovering
and bedlinen ranges with classic
and contemporary designs.
Tel: 01895 830000
www.sanderson-uk.com

WILMAN INTERIORS
Contemporary and classic
fabrics and wallpapers.
Tel: 01282 727300
www.wilman.co.uk

AMERICAN SHUTTERS
Custom-made wooden
shutters painted or stained
in the colour of your choice.
Tel: 020 8876 5905

ARTISAN
Wide range of poles and finials,
from trendy to traditional in
style.
Tel: 01772 203555

THE BRADLEY COLLECTION
Stylish curtain poles and
finials in wood and sleek
steel.
Tel: 01449 722724
www.bradleycollection.co.uk

THE CURTAIN EXCHANGE
Quality secondhand curtains
bought and sold.
Tel: 020 7731 8316
www.thecurtainexchange.cwc.
net

ECLECTICS
Made-to-measure and ready-
made roller and Roman blinds
in smart modern designs.
Tel: 0870 010 2211
www.eclectics.co.uk

MARKS & SPENCER
Curtains and blinds, poles and
tiebacks.
Tel: 020 7935 4422 for stockists,
0845 603 1603 for mail order
www.marks-and-spencer.com

WINDOW
TREATMENTS

PRÊT À VIVRE
Curtains and blinds made to
measure; poles and tiebacks.
Tel: 020 8960 6111
www.pretavivre.com

ROSEBYS
Ready-made curtains and blinds.
Tel: 0115 925 5999
www.rosebys.com

RUFFLETTE
Tiebacks, blind and eyelet kits
and curtain-making products.
Tel: 0161 998 1811
www.rufflette.com

THE SHUTTER SHOP
Wooden shutters made to order;
wooden Venetian blinds.
Tel: 01252 844575
www.shuttershop.co.uk

VELUX
Skylight windows for loft rooms
and blinds designed to fit them.
Tel: 0800 316 8822
www.velux.co.uk

FIREPLACES
AND FITTINGS

AMAZING GRATES
Reproduction period fireplaces
in marble, stone and slate.
Tel: 020 8883 9590
www.amazing-grates.co.uk

CLAYTON MUNROE
Period-style door handles.
Tel: 01803 762626
www.claytonmunroe.co.uk

ELGIN & HALL
Made-to-order fireplaces in a
wide range of styles.
Tel: 01677 450100
www.elgin.co.uk

HAF DESIGNS
Contemporary door handles in
steel and brass.
Tel: 01992 505655
www.hafdesigns.co.uk

JALI
MDF fittings made to measure,
including radiator covers,
shelving, pelmets and screens.
Tel: 01227 831710
www.jali.co.uk

KNOBS & KNOCKERS
Door furniture in modern and traditional designs.
Tel: 0151 523 4900
www.knobsandknockers.co.uk

PECO
Vast choice of original and reproduction doors and fully restored fireplaces.
Tel: 020 8979 8310

RICHARD BURBIDGE
Wooden mouldings for dado rails and panel effects.
Tel: 01691 678201
www.richardburbidge.co.uk

TURNSTYLE DESIGNS
Handcrafted door handles made from resin, pewter and wood.
Tel: 01271 325325

WINTHER BROWNE
Simple fire surrounds in pine, mahogany and MDF; flatpack ready-to-paint radiator cabinets.
Tel: 020 8803 3434

ALLIED CARPETS
Carpet superstores with a wide range of colours and patterns.
Tel: 08000 932932

BRINTONS
Vast range of Axminster and Wilton carpets.
Tel: 0800 505055
www.brintons.co.uk

CRUCIAL TRADING
Natural floorcoverings and rugs in sisal, coir and seagrass.
Tel: 01562 825656
www.crucial-trading.com

JUNCKERS
Solid hardwood flooring in oak, beech and ash.
Tel: 01376 534705
www.junckers.dk

KÄHRS FLOORING
Hardwood flooring mostly from sustainable Swedish forests.
Tel: 01243 778747
www.kahrs.se

PERGO ORIGINAL
Wood-effect laminate flooring.
Tel: 0800 374771
www.pergo.com

FLOORING

THE RUG COMPANY
Handmade quality rugs from around the world.
Tel: 020 7229 5148
www.rugcompany.co.uk

RYALUX CARPETS
Plain and subtly patterned wool carpets that can be supplied in any width to avoid wastage.
Tel: 0800 163632
www.ryalux.carpetinfo.co.uk

TOMKINSONS CARPETS
Wide range of colours and patterns, plus jazzy borders.
Tel: 0800 374429

LIGHTING

BHS
Stylish but affordable lights and shades in a range of styles.
Tel: 020 7262 3288
www.bhs.co.uk

CHRISTOPHER WRAY LIGHTING
Huge range of designs, from cutting-edge to traditional, including many chandeliers.
Tel: 020 7736 8434
www.christopher-wray.com

HABITAT
Modern light fittings in chrome and glass; paper shades in many shapes and sizes.
Tel: 0845 601 0740
www.habitat.net

IKEA
Contemporary designs, including very affordable table lamps.
Tel: 020 8208 5600

LAURA ASHLEY
Varied choice of classic and country-style lights and lamps.
Tel: 0870 562 2116 for stockists, 0800 868100 for mail order

MCCLOUD & CO
Vast choice of light fittings by British craftspeople, available in a selection of different finishes.
Tel: 020 7352 1533
www.mccloud.co.uk

PURVES & PURVES
Contemporary light fittings by
top European designers, plus
some more affordable designs.
Tel: 020 7580 8223
www.purves.co.uk

SKK LIGHTS
Innovative light fittings, including some wacky designs.
Tel: 020 7434 4095
www.skk.net

THE STIFFKEY LAMPSHOP
Original and reproduction lamps,
candlesticks and candelabra.
Tel: 01328 830460

WAX LYRICAL
Decorative candles and candle-
holders.
Tel: 020 8561 0235
www.waxlyrical.co.uk

BEDLINEN AND ACCESSORIES

BEDECK
Bedlinen featuring modern
florals and geometric
patterns.
Tel: 0845 603 0861
www.bedeckhome.com

BLISS
Accessories with quirky shapes,
such as clocks.
Tel: 01789 400077

BOMBAY DUCK
Decorative contemporary
accessories, including photo
frames and beaded items.
Tel: 020 8749 7000
www.bombayduck.co.uk

COLOGNE & COTTON
Crisp cotton bedlinen and pretty
duvet covers.
Tel: 01926 332573

THE COTSWOLD COMPANY
Country-style storage baskets in
wicker and rattan.
Tel: 01252 391404
www.cotswoldco.com

COUVERTURE
Hand-embroidered and
appliquéd bedlinen.
Tel: 020 7795 1200

DESCAMPS
Quality bedlinen, including modern patterns and florals.
Tel: 020 7235 6957
www.descamps.com

DORMA
Varied range of bedlinen, from elaborately classic to plain contemporary designs.
Tel: 0161 251 4468 for stockists, 0870 606 6063 for brochure

THE HAMBLEDON
Stylish accessories, including simple vases and cotton quilts.
Tel: 01962 890055

LAKELAND LIMITED
Storage fittings for organising wardrobe and drawer space.
Tel: 015394 88100
www.lakelandlimited.co.uk

MCCORD DESIGN BY MAIL
Contemporary bedlinen and varied cushion collection.
Tel: 0870 908 7005
www.emccord.com

MARKS & SPENCER
Classic and modern bedlinen and bedroom accessories.
Tel: 020 7935 4422 for stockists, 0845 603 1603 for mail order
www.marks-and-spencer.com

MELIN TREGWYNT
Traditional Welsh blankets and throws in pure wool and angora.
Tel: 01348 891644

MONSOON HOME
Embroidered throws and cushions in colourful silks.
Tel: 020 7313 3000
www.monsoon.co.uk

MUJI
Minimalist storage accessories made from cardboard, polypropylene and steel.
Tel: 020 7323 2208

OCEAN
Contemporary bedlinen, cushions and throws.
Tel: 0870 242 6283
www.oceanupstairs.com

PEACOCK BLUE
Cotton and linen bedding including whites, ginghams and pastels.
Tel: 0870 333 1555
www.peacockblue.co.uk

THE WHITE COMPANY
Plain and embroidered bedlinen in white and cream made from top-quality linen and cotton.
Tel: 0870 160 1610

YVES DELORME
Luxury French bedlinen in classic and contemporary styles.
Tel: 01296 394980
www.yvesdelorme.com

BRITISH BLIND & SHUTTER ASSOCIATION

Information and advice on where to buy blinds and shutters.
01827 52337
www.bbsa.co.uk

THE BRITISH CARPET MANUFACTURERS' ASSOCIATION

Free booklets giving advice on choosing and caring for carpets.
Tel: 01562 747351

THE BRITISH DECORATORS' ASSOCIATION

Can supply a list of decorators in your area and a leaflet advising how to choose one.
Tel: 01203 353776

THE BUILDING CENTRE

Building information and advice; DIY guides available to buy; free reference library.
Tel: 020 7692 6200
www.buildingcentre.co.uk

THE LIGHTING ASSOCIATION

Advice on where to find answers to lighting queries; free buyers' guide available.
Tel: 01952 290905

NATIONAL INSTITUTE OF CARPET AND FLOOR LAYERS

Help with finding the right professionals to fit flooring.
Tel: 0115 958 3077

THE ROYAL INSTITUTE OF BRITISH ARCHITECTS

Can send out lists of member architects in your area.
Tel: 020 7580 5533

SALVO

Information on local salvage yards available for a small fee.
Tel: 01890 820333
www.salvo.co.uk

THE SLEEP COUNCIL

Leaflets and advice on how to choose and buy a bed.
Tel: 01756 79237

ADVICE

SAVE 28% when you

BBC Good Homes

Now that you have had a taste of *Good Homes* inspiration why not take this opportunity to receive accessible ideas and design all year round by subscribing to *BBC Good Homes magazine* for only £9.99! Every issue of *BBC Good Homes magazine* is packed with the freshest ideas in home décor with

SUBSCRIBER BENEFITS

- Free delivery
- Avoid any future cover price increases

all the advice you need to re-create them in your own home, plus property news, readers' homes and makeovers.

To take advantage of this exclusive 6 month